Memory for Forgetfulness

August, Beirut, 1982

| | | | |

LITERATURE OF THE MIDDLE EAST
a series of fiction, poetry, and memoirs
in translation

Memory
for Forgetfulness
August, Beirut, 1982

Mahmoud Darwish

*Translated, with an Introduction
by Ibrahim Muhawi*

University of California Press
Berkeley | *Los Angeles* | *London*

Library of Congress Cataloging-in-Publication Data
Darwish, Maḥmūd
[Dhākirah lil-nisyān. English]
Memory for forgetfulness : August, Beirut, 1982 / Mahmoud Darwish; trans-
lated, with an introduction by Ibrahim Muhawi.
p.   cm.
Includes bibliographical references.
ISBN 0-520-08767-4 (alk. paper).—ISBN 0-520-08768-2 (pbk. :
alk. paper)
I. Lebanon—History—Israeli intervention, 1982-1984—Personal
narratives, Palestinian.   2. Beirut (Lebanon)—History.   3. Darwish,
Maḥmūd.   I. Muhawi, Ibrahim, 1937–.   II. Title.
DS87.53.D36513   1982
956.9204'4—dc20   94-26351

University of California Press
Berkeley and Los Angeles, California

University of California Press, Ltd.
London, England

The original Arabic edition of this work appeared in *Al
Karmel*, nos. 21–22 (1986): 4–96. *Al Karmel* is the journal of
the General Union of Palestinian Writers and Journalists (al-
Ittiḥād al-ʿĀmm li-l-Kuttāb wa al-Ṣaḥafiyyīn al-Filasṭīniyyīn).
It is published by Bisan Press (Muʾassasat Bīsān li-l-Ṣaḥāfah
wa al-Nashr wa al-Tawzīʿ), 4 Churchill Street, P.O. Box 4256,
Nicosia, Cyprus. The Arabic title of the work is *Dhakirah li-l-
nisyān*.

Printed in the United States of America

08   07   06   05   04   03   02
9   8   7   6

C'est précisément parce que j'oublie que je lis.

Roland Barthes

Contents

| | | | | |

Acknowledgments

| | | | | | | | | | |

I would like to express my gratitude to the following people, without whose contribution this work would not be what it is.

To Emna Moalla, my colleague at the Faculté des Lettres de la Manouba (Université de Tunis—I), for giving unstintingly of her time in checking various drafts of the translation against the original. Her mastery of both Arabic and English is such as to inspire confidence; and, with a work like this one, this mastery was needed.

To Sheila Levine, of UC Press, for initial encouragement to proceed.

To Lynne Withey and Stephanie Fay, my present editors at UC Press, for dedicated enthusiasm, follow-up, and care with the manuscript; and to the editorial staff at UC Press, who continue to uphold the standard of excellence in book production.

To Ahmad Dahbour, a Palestinian poet and friend of Darwish, for being there when needed.

To my good friend, Nasreddine Hajjaj, a Palestinian writer and son of Ain Hilwe refugee camp in South Lebanon, for helping to see this work through and for providing invaluable assistance.

To Jane Muhawi, my wife and native ear, I owe more than I know how to put into words. Without her unfailing encouragement and her commitment, this work might never have been finished. And without her mastery of English, her native tongue, and her priceless literacy, the translation would not sound as it does.

Introduction

| | | | | | |

In the Arab world Mahmoud Darwish is acknowledged as one of the greatest living poets. He has been awarded a number of international literary prizes, and has read his poetry to audiences in many countries around the world. When he gives a reading in any Arab country today, his audience runs into the thousands, with many people turned away for lack of space. He has so far published fourteen volumes of poetry, the first of which, *Olive Leaves*, appeared in 1964, and the latest, *Eleven Planets*, in 1993. His *Diwan*, or collected poems, comprising the first nine volumes, has been reprinted numerous times. He also has seven prose works to his name, including this one. Many poems and articles published in various magazines, as well as a number of television and newspaper interviews, have not yet been collected. Selections from his poetry have appeared in translation in at least twenty languages, but, considering his stature, he is not as well known in the English-speaking world as he should be.

This work, *Memory for Forgetfulness (Dha:kira li-l-nisya:n)*, which grew out of the Israeli invasion of Lebanon that began on 6 June 1982, originally appeared in 1986, under the title *The Time: Beirut / The Place: August*, in *Al Karmel*, the prestigious literary quarterly Darwish has edited since 1981.[1] It was later published under its present title in Beirut and Rabat, the Beirut edition using the original title as subtitle. Aside from the addition of a few breaks, the text translated here is the one that appeared in *Al Karmel;* I have followed the Arabic as closely as I could without sacrificing fluency.

Mahmoud Darwish was born in the village of Birwe, district of Acre, in Upper Galilee on 13 March 1942. In 1948, after its inhabitants, including the child and his family, had fled to Lebanon, the newly formed Israel destroyed the village. Darwish's family, as he tells us in the book, stole back into the homeland, but too late to be included in the census of the Palestinian Arabs who had remained in the country. Until 1966 the Palestinian Arab citizens of Israel were under military rule and subject to a complex set of emergency regulations, including one that required them to secure a permit for travel inside the country. Lacking identity papers, the poet was vulnerable and was kept under constant watch by the Israeli military. Between 1961 and 1969 he was imprisoned and put under house arrest several times. He had not committed any crimes other than writing poetry and traveling without a permit inside the country: "For the first time they'd given us permission to leave Haifa, but we had to be back at night to report to the police station. . . . 'Put this in your record: I'm present!' " The rhythmic return to the poet's

---

1. Nos. 21–22 (1986):4–96. I have used the accepted transliterated spelling for Arabic names but for other words have adopted a more accurate system, as follows: emphatic consonants are rendered in capitals; the voiced pharyngeal fricative, with a question mark; the voiceless, with H; the glottal stop, with an apostrophe; the voiced dental fricative with "dh"; the voiceless palatal fricative, with "sh"; the voiced uvular fricative, with "gh"; the voiceless, with a "kh"; and long vowels, by means of a following colon.

life in the homeland, including the periods of restricted move-
ment, forms the pole of memory in the text, while the events
surrounding the invasion of Lebanon and the siege of Beirut
form the pole of forgetfulness.

Nearly ten years earlier, in *Journal of an Ordinary Grief*
(*Yawmiyya:t al-Huzn al-ʔa:di:* [1973], p. 94), Darwish had de-
scribed Palestinian existence under Israeli rule as a paradox:

> You want to travel to Greece? You ask for a passport,
> but you discover you're not a citizen because your father
> or one of your relatives had fled with you during the Pales-
> tine war. You were a child. And you discover that any
> Arab who had left his country during that period and had
> stolen back in had lost his right to citizenship.
>
> You despair of the passport and ask for a laissez-passer.
> You find out you're not a resident of Israel because you
> have no certificate of residence. You think it's a joke and
> rush to tell it to your lawyer friend: "Here, I'm not a citi-
> zen, and I'm not a resident. Then where and who am I?"
> You're surprised to find the law is on their side, and you
> must prove you exist. You ask the Ministry of the Interior,
> "Am I here, or am I absent? Give me an expert in philoso-
> phy, so that I can prove to him I exist."
>
> Then you realize that philosophically you exist but
> legally you do not.

In 1971 Darwish left Israel for Cairo, where he worked for
the leading Egyptian daily, *Al Ahram.* In 1973 he joined the Pal-
estine Liberation Organization as assistant to the director of the
Palestine Research Center in Beirut, and helped edit its scholarly
journal, *Shu'u:n FilasTi:niya (Palestinian Affairs).* Soon after, he

became the director of the center and chief editor of the journal. In 1984, while still recuperating from the heart attack he alludes to in this work, he was unanimously elected president of the Union of Palestinian Writers and Journalists. And in 1987 he became a member of the highest Palestinian decision-making body, the PLO Executive Committee, from which he resigned on 13 September 1993, when the government of Israel and the Palestine Liberation Organization signed a "Declaration of Principles on Interim Self-Government Arrangements" (otherwise known as "Gaza-Jericho First")—not necessarily because he opposed it, but because he did not want to be held responsible "for this risky accord." "My role on the Executive Committee," he said, "was that of a symbol. I was there to provide a moderating influence on the tension and to help reconcile differences. I have never been a man of politics. I am a poet with a particular perspective on reality."[2]

The historical background to *Memory for Forgetfulness* is the siege of Beirut ("the small island of the spirit") in 1982. For more than two months, from 14 June to 23 August, the Israelis and their Phalangist supporters surrounded and besieged the Palestinian resistance and their nationalist Lebanese allies. In 1985, three years after the Palestinian leadership were driven out and the Israeli army entered the city, Darwish isolated himself in his Paris apartment for ninety days or so, and wrote with a passionate commitment this masterpiece of Arabic literature. Its form is that of a memoir, the record of a single day on the streets of Beirut when bombardment from land, sea, and air was one of the most intensive a city had ever known. The *Sunday Times*

2. *Al-Qods Al-Arabi*, 17 November 1993.

of London for 8 August 1982 quoted a cable sent to the State Department by then U.S. Ambassador to Lebanon Robert S. Dillon: "Simply put, tonight's saturation shelling was as intense as anything we have seen. There was no 'pinpoint accuracy' against targets in 'open spaces.' It was not a response to Palestinian fire. This was a blitz against West Beirut."

Extraordinary conditions foreground the ordinary, and the heroic consists in living every moment to the full. With shells exploding everywhere, the effort to maintain the primacy of the quotidian becomes a challenge to the bombs, and an ordinary task like making coffee turns into a meditation on the aesthetics of hand movement and the art of combining different ingredients to create something new. In a conversation with me in Tunis in April 1993, Darwish said that although Palestinian writing had not dared admit to fear, his own text was an attempt to confront the fact of fear, the violence and the destruction. By calmly carrying on with daily routines, one could defy the onslaught and take hold of oneself. Sheer survival during a blitz assumes heroic proportions, and a walk on the streets of the city that apocalyptic day, 6 August 1982, Hiroshima Day, becomes an odyssey.

The book opens with the author waking at dawn from a dream and closes with him going to sleep at the end of the day. To describe his state of being in the paradise collapsing all around him, he identifies himself with Adam, the original epic hero of human history: "I didn't know my name, or the name of this place. . . . What is my name? Who gave me my name? Who is going to call me Adam?" An accomplished poet could not treat an event of this magnitude as an ordinary event, as did the news announcers on the BBC and Radio Monte Carlo whom

Darwish mocks: " 'Intensive bombardment of Beirut.' *Intensive bombardment of Beirut!* Is this aired as an ordinary news item about an ordinary day in an ordinary war in an ordinary newscast?" Understandably, he wanted to write about it in an extraordinary way that reflected the existential situation of a people whose history since 1948 has been a nightmare from which there has been no waking.

To convey the magnitude of the invasion and the siege, the pole of forgetfulness, the poet puts the act of writing itself under siege, lest the magic power of words seduce readers into a comfortable relationship with the text, just as the Palestinian Movement itself misread Lebanon and was seduced into an easy relation with it in which the basic assumption was false: "We write the script and the dialogue; we design the scenario; we pick the actors, the cameraman, the director, and the producer; and we distribute the roles without realizing we're the ones cast in them." Even death is not real unless it is borne witness to in writing: "The one looking for a paper in the midst of this hell is running from a solitary, to a collective death. . . . He's looking for some kind of participation in this death, for a witness [*sha:hid*] who can give evidence, for a gravestone over a corpse." Existence itself in the Arab and Islamic view, as the segment from Ibn Athir confirms, is understood through the metaphor of writing: "Then God . . . created the Pen and commanded it, so that it wrote into being everything that will exist till the Day of Judgment."

What Darwish attempts is a pure gesture in which writing itself becomes the dominant metaphor. He offers us a multivocal text that resembles a broken mirror, reassembled to present the viewer with vying possibilities of clarity and fracture. On the page different kinds of writing converge: the poem, both verse and prose; dialogue; Scripture; history; myth; myth in the guise of history; narrative fiction; literary criticism; and dream visions. Each segment can stand on its own, yet each acquires a relational or a dialectical meaning, a history, that is contingent upon the context provided for it by all the other segments of the work. As we move forward in the text, we are at the same time moving vertically through all these different kinds of writing, and back and forth in time. Thus the segment on Hiroshima creates a context for an apocalyptic interpretation of Beirut during the siege.[3] Although this inclusiveness reflects breakdown, it also embodies a synthesis. Suspended between wholeness and fracture, the text, like Palestine, is a crossroads of competing meanings.

Homeland is to keep alive the memory, Darwish says in *Journal of an Ordinary Grief,* and to the extent that this book accomplishes that, it too is a kind of homeland and the experi-

---

3. Cf. David Gilmour, *Dispossessed: The Ordeal of the Palestinians* (London: Sphere Books, 1982), pp. 223–24:

> The bombardment of Beirut was one of the most horrific events of recent history. Day after day Israeli gunners sat outside the city lobbing thousands of shells into the densely packed apartment blocks. From the sea the Israeli navy pounded the coastal districts while F16 aeroplanes screeched overhead terrorizing the population and levelling whole buildings. According to the *Sunday Times* [8 August 1982] among the targets hit by the Israelis in the two months following their arrival in Beirut were "five UN buildings, a hundred and thirty-four embassies or diplomatic residences, six hospitals or clinics, one mental institute, the Central Bank, five hotels, the Red Cross, Lebanese and foreign media outlets and innumerable private homes." Apart from the six thousand PLO guerillas in the besieged city, there were some half million Lebanese and Palestinian civilians, and every day of the bombardment about two hundred or three hundred of them were killed. Many of them were burned to death by phosphorus bombs. The Canadian ambassador, Theodore Arcand, said [*Sunday Times,* 8 August 1982] that the destruction was so comprehensive it "would make Berlin of 1945 look like a tea party."

ence of reading it represents a return. Engaging readers directly in the creation of this meaning, the text remains, in the terms proposed by Umberto Eco, an "open work," in which every reception is "both an *interpretation* and a *performance* [emphasis in original]."[4]

Meaning has no closure here, just as the historical experience of the Palestinian people in its present phase has no closure. For example, although the dream that opens the book is mysterious at first, its relevance unfolds at strategic intervals until its significance to the structure of the work as a whole is revealed. This way reading becomes a constant unfolding of meaning, and both belief and disbelief must remain suspended and open to the resolution of the various narratives woven together in the text, with a return to the homeland, the originary text and source of meaning, remaining a possibility. "In its essence," Darwish says in the opening words to *Journal of an Ordinary Grief,* "writing remains the other shape of the homeland."

To the extent that Darwish combines the private voice with the public, his personal experience reflects the collective experience of the Palestinian people. Our first encounter with the Palestinian paradox in this work is in the title, *Memory for Forgetfulness.* The deceptively simple preposition obscures as much as it reveals. His initial intention when he first set himself to the task, Darwish said, was to write down the recurring dream that opens and closes the work, and haunts it throughout. But to his surprise, he produced a long text about the Beirut phase of the Palestinian experience, *tajribat* Beirut. Thus writing the

4. Umberto Eco, *The Role of the Reader* (Bloomington: Indiana University Press, 1979), p. 49.

book was for him a recollection in tranquillity, a use of memory *for the purpose of* forgetfulness, for purging the violent emotions attached to the events described. The poet wanted to forget. But for the reader the poet's recollection is transformed into a text and his purgation becomes an act of memory, a monument, *against* forgetfulness and the ravages of history.

Seeing the invasion and the siege, which meant the departure of the Palestinian idea from Beirut, as a final attempt to ensure a collective amnesia about Palestine, the poet chose to join battle against oblivion. This choice recalls Hölderlin's line: *"Was bleibet aber / Stiften die Dichter"* (But that which remains / Is established by the poets).[5] It is no surprise that Darwish, as an artist, should translate the Palestinian experience of war and siege into universal terms, that he should link history and art, for as the Italian philosopher Gianni Vattimo explains, the work of art, in opening a historical horizon, is an enactment (a setting-into-work) of the truth: there is no truth without history. The work of art "is the act by which a certain historical and cultural world is instituted, in which a specific historical 'humanity' sees the characteristic traits of its own experience of the world defined in an originary way."[6]

The relationship of the book to Palestinian history is not so clear-cut, however, for the title raises the question of destiny, or historical inevitability. The title's preposition reifies the abstract nouns on either side of it and unites them in a relationship of part to whole. Forgetfulness here is not personal and private, but a fact of history, an infinite horizon of blue nothingness,

5. Quoted in Gianni Vattimo, *The End of Modernity*, trans. Jon R. Snyder (Cambridge, England: Polity Press, 1988), p. 66.

6. Ibid., p. 66.

and writing is like the ship with the Palestinians aboard, making its way into an unknown and inscribing its course in its own wake. Since *memory* refers among other things both to Palestine ("And the sung beauty, the object of worship, has moved away to a memory now joining battle against the fangs of a forgetfulness made of steel") and to the Palestinian people ("Memory doesn't remember but receives the history raining down on it"), this reading carries fearful implications, suggesting perhaps the author's dread that the dream of the return will not be realized, that the Palestinians may remain in exile, falling victim to history and joining the long caravans of oblivion: "I don't see a shore. I don't see a dove."

Meditation on the relationship of writing to history has engaged many writers. The monumental aspect of writing also engages Eliot in *Four Quartets* : "Every phrase and every sentence is an end and a beginning, / Every poem an epitaph" ("Little Gidding"). Every segment in Darwish's text is both an end and a beginning. In the monumental dimension of the book, which can be seen as a memorial to the resistance of the Lebanese and Palestinian people, the poet also puts his signature on the landscape of history: "I want a language that I can lean on and that can lean on me, that asks me to bear witness and that I can ask to bear witness." The Arabic root meaning "bearing witness," *shahida*, also produces "gravestone" or "epitaph," *sha:hid*, and "martyr," *shahi:d*—words that echo throughout the work. Here, writing is history's witness, its epitaph: both *sha:hid*.

When the act of writing is conscripted as metaphor, the text loses its stability. In conversation Darwish has described his text as *mutawattir* (nervous, tense, taut, on edge). It was an attempt to get the Lebanese phase of Palestinian history, the madness that was Beirut (*junu:n Beirut,* also meaning "possession by Beirut"), and his attachment to the city out of his system. Once he had finished, he sent it to the publisher. He has not read it since. In "Burnt Norton," T. S. Eliot says:

Words strain
Crack and sometimes break, under the burden,
Under the tension, slip, slide, perish,
Decay with imprecision, will not stay in place,
Will not stay still.

These lines suggest what Darwish meant by *mutawattir* and describe his technique in the text.

The contingency of all life under bombardment is embodied in the words that crack and break in Darwish's nervous text, what Vattimo calls "the shattering of the poetic word in the originary saying of poetry." "The anticipation of death, upon which the possibility of authentic existence depends," Vattimo explains, "is the experience of the connection between language and mortality."[7] In the midst of the overwhelming actuality of death, Darwish sets down, in his poetic prose, moments of authentic existence. We may thus conceive of the text as a relation between poetic language and mortality; death, in the aesthetic transformation of reality into art, becomes a metaphor intrinsic to the work.

By restricting the frame of reference to a geographical area and a historical event, the original title, however paradoxical its equation of time and place, could lead to a misreading of the book solely in terms of the geography and the event. The pres-

7. Ibid., p. 70.

ent, more general, title discloses Darwish's method of composition and articulates the work's complex existence as a text, or memory, in relation to the world. The poet uses irony and paradox to render Palestinian historical experience in an immediate and dramatic manner: "For the first time in our history, our absence is conditional upon our total presence. Present to make oneself absent." This is reminiscent of the bitterly ironic "present-absent," Israel's label for internal refugees, away from their villages at the time the state was established, whose lands it wanted to confiscate. Palestinians, present in their absence, are themselves a memory preserved against forgetfulness. Like Palestinian existence, the book itself may be described as an extended oxymoron.

During the shelling the extent of the entire Arab homeland shrinks—to Lebanon, to the city of Beirut, to a quarter in that city, to a street, to a building which has just been hit, to a room within that building (say, the author's study), and finally by implication to the printed page where these events are taking place in the reader's imagination: "What am I searching for? I open the door several times, but find no newspaper. Why am I looking for the paper when buildings are falling in all directions? Is that not writing enough?" In this ironic exchange of roles, the text becomes the world, and the world, the text. The page is here equated with the landscape and becomes the mimetic space where negation is negated and forgetfulness is to be forgotten by means of writing. Thus the print medium also acts as a metaphor, the printed page as an icon of the action, as if the exploding shell burst into fragments of discourse on the page, just as the actual shell reconfigures the city's landscape.

Considering the paucity of material resources available to

the defenders of Beirut, the ironic mode is the only available answer to the overstatement of the bombs falling on the city during the siege, a response that pits one kind of power against another. By an exercise of the imagination the poet equates the unequatable, words and ordnance: "I want to find a language that transforms language itself into steel for the spirit—a language to use against these sparkling silver insects, these jets." This aspect of the work is carried in the title preposition's suggestion of an exchange, as in *blow for blow*—as if the author were saying, "You give me bombs, I give you a text"; "You give me forgetfulness, I give you memory"; or "You give me history, I give you writing."[8]

Appropriately, metaphors of explosion and fusion recur in the text: memory fusing into forgetfulness, which in turn forgets

8. The ironic view of Palestinian history is not limited to Mahmoud Darwish. Emile Habiby, the major Palestinian novelist, is also ironic in his vision, as is clearly illustrated by the title of his most important work, "The Strange Events Concerning the Disappearance of Said ('The Happy One') Son of Misfortune, the Optipessimist." This work is available in English as *The Secret Life of Saeed, the Ill-Fated Pessoptimist: A Palestinian Who Became a Citizen of Israel,* trans. Salma Jayyusi and Trevor Le Gassick (New York: Vantage Press, 1982).

Edward Said reflects on Palestinian history from the same perspective. In a recent article he says, "What to many Palestinians is either an incomprehensible cruelty of fate or a measure of how appalling are the prospects for settling their claim can be clarified by seeing irony as a constitutive factor in their lives." To speak of recent Palestinian history in the aesthetic terms of irony, he affirms, "is by no means to reduce or trivialize its force." More specifically, Palestinian history is characterized by "irony and paradox" in its relation to the Arab states—an aspect of Palestinian existence to which Darwish devotes some of his most trenchant comments in this work. And, most significantly in terms of Darwish's project in *Memory,* Palestinian history is also characterized by irony in the encounter with Israel: "Here, then, is another complex irony: how the classic victims of years of anti-semitic persecution and Holocaust have in their nation become the victimizers of another people, who have become therefore the victims of the victims." See Said's "Reflections on Twenty Years of Palestinian History," *Journal of Palestine Studies,* no. 80 (Summer 1991): 5, 15.

itself and bursts into memory: "If only one of us would forget the other so that forgetfulness itself might be stricken with memory!" In time, fusion is one thing and explosion, another, but at the moment of creation fusion and explosion unite, giving birth to the text and the present. The threat of imminent death collapses time to the interval between two shells, which is shorter than the instant "between breathing in and breathing out." These "moments/spasms," instants of creation when time and space collapse into each other, are also moments for the maximum release of energy.

The erotic element in the book, which metaphorically equates love and death, is a necessary counterpart to mortality that, as we have seen, also generates metaphors for the activities of writing and reading: "The obscure heaps up on the obscure, rubs against itself, and ignites into clarity." To spark this clarity, the text characteristically places the reader at a meeting point, a point of reversal, a juxtaposition, whether of two segments of the text or two (or more) perspectives. For example, in the first two sentences of the book the discourse shifts from direct statement to dialogue (I have indicated these shifts with italics). Immediately thereafter comes a reversal of ordinary assumptions about birth, love, life, and death: "Because you woke me up when you stirred in my belly. I knew then I was your coffin." To be born is to die. Memory is *for* forgetfulness; it exists to be forgotten.

The rhythm of reversal that weaves the text together is rooted in historical experience, reflecting the departure of the Palestinian leadership from Lebanon in 1982, and the earlier exit from Palestine in 1948. With that exit, which turned a settled population into refugees, reality itself was reversed and the words became hollow shells without meaning in the Arab waste-land (the "desert" and "wilderness" in the text), forcing the Pal-estinians to reverse the process of intellectual, political, and spiritual degeneration that has taken hold of the Arabs: "From now on we have nothing to lose, so long as Beirut is here and we're here in Beirut as names for a different homeland, where meanings will find their words again in the midst of this sea and on the edge of this desert." In the text this rhythm of reversal emerges in a whole lexicon of words born from other words (nouns, verbs, verbal nouns), all meaning "exit" (e.g., *kharaja* and its variants). The departure from Beirut; the exit from Pales-tine; the birth of the dream from the dream, of the text from the dream, of the words from each other, and of the textual seg-ments from each other are all united in this rhythm. A subsid-iary rhythm based on the use of symbol also emerges as words like *rain, wave, sea, island, desert, birth, death, graveyard, knight, horse, poem, white* are repeated to give a mythic dimension to events. The wave that propels the Palestinian ship in its journey to the unknown, for example, also joins Beirut and Haifa—two jewels on the sea—for which the author harbors an inordinate love, and Palestine and Andalusia, two "lost paradises," or loci of meaning.

As we have seen, Darwish's artistic purpose in this work is in part to revitalize language by bringing meaning back to the words, or by endowing them with new meanings. The invasion ultimately will mean yet another journey for the Palestinian peo-ple, a journey across the sea—*al-baHr*. But *al-baHr* is also the word used for the meter, or poetic measure, of Arabic prosody. When a fighter wants to know the difference between the sea in poetry and the actual sea, the poet answers, "The *sea* is the sea."

The sea is itself; it is also poetic measure. Poetic measure is itself; it is also the sea. Further, there is no difference between them. Language, like Palestine, unites what can't be united, and meaning cuts across the boundaries separating world and text.

The man of politics, or the poet? In the shift from the original to the present title the poet signaled that the book is to be read as a work of literature, a "setting-into-work of truth," that opens out a horizon on the history of the Palestinian people through the optic of an invasion meant to negate their identity and the facts of their history. To the extent that it does this successfully—that is, to the extent that it succeeds as a work of art—it is a supremely political document, and not the other way around, as many of his readers would have it. That he had long been acclaimed as a leading writer and the national poet of Palestine he himself acknowledges in passages of this book: "And if we complain of the general inability to perfect a language of the people in creative expression, that should not prevent us from insisting on speaking for them until the moment arrives when literature can celebrate its great wedding, when the private voice and the public voice become one."

Darwish insists on his identity as a poet, albeit one who has espoused the Palestinian national cause. His early poem "Identity Card" was his way of saying, "I exist," despite his lack of papers. The poem shot him to prominence among the Palestinians in Israel and in the larger Arab world as well and, along with other early poems, earned him the simplistic label of resistance poet. As he is about to go to sleep at the end of that endless day of bombing, in the moments of reverie that bring the book to a close, he recalls that poem: ". . . an old rhythm I recognize! . . . I recognize this voice, whose age was twenty five . . .

'Put this in your record: I'm Arab!' " Here, past and present melt into each other: "This outcry then became my poetic identity, which has not been satisfied with pointing to my father but chases me even now."

Clearly, the question of this identity—that is, how he is read—has haunted Darwish. For many years now he has made it his task to kill this "father," to combat the critical straightjacket into which he has been forced by Arab as well as Western critics who have consistently (mis)read him politically as a resistance poet, or as a poet of the (Palestinian) Resistance, rather than a poet whose major concerns are national. In an interview first published in *Al Karmel* and later in *Al-Qods Al-Arabi*, he addresses this issue again:

> A poem exists only in the relation between poet and reader. And I'm in need of my readers, except that they never cease to write me as they would wish, turning their reading into another writing that almost rubs out my features. I don't know why my poetry has to be killed on the altar of misunderstanding or the fallacy of ready-made intent. I am not solely a citizen of Palestine, though I am proud of this affiliation and ready to sacrifice my life in defending the radiance of the Palestinian fact, but I also want to take up the history of my people and their struggle from an aesthetic angle that differs from the prevalent and repeatable meanings readily available from an unmediated political reading.[9]

When I asked him whether he thought the text was poetry or prose, Darwish replied that the poet is always a poet; he re-

9. *Al Karmel*, no. 47 (1993): 140; *Al-Qods Al-Arabi*, 12 February 1993.

mains true to himself whatever he does, in life or letters. He pays attention to rhythm and other verse values in all his writings. Therefore, he, Darwish, does not distinguish aesthetically between poetry and prose and takes equal care in the form and content of all his writings. So although the work belongs more properly to poetry than to prose because it was written by a poet, we can say, since its form is prose, that it partakes of the nature of both: with the exception of the segment on literary criticism, it is a collection of prose poems. Darwish himself gives us a clue to this effect in his description of Beirut as "a musical name which can flow smoothly into a verse or a prose poem," and in his reference to his friend the older poet who was the first writer to write the prose poem in Arabic.

To help him with this scheme, the author draws upon the grammar of the language. Reading in Arabic is not the same process as it is in English, where the movement of the attention from left to right is unhampered. Because diacritical marks, or voweling, are normally not inserted in printed Arabic texts, grammatical relationships are not immediately apparent. Meaning is deferred, and readers are forced to move back and forth within the same sentence. This in part explains Darwish's practice of writing long ambiguous sentences, with multiple levels of meaning. Further, because Arabic has no tense as such, grammatical time is not, as in English, defined in relation to the moment of speech, a process that interjects an implied subject in every utterance. Arabic prose does not have to maintain the consistent pattern of tense sequence required in English. Hence it is easy for Darwish to scramble time, removing the action from the temporal sphere and placing it in a dreamlike realm. In the translation I adopted the author's journey on the streets of Beirut, in the present tense, as the reference point for the action.

In his attempt to make the work a perfect portrait of Palestinian experience, Darwish needed a form that could free him from the constraints imposed by form itself. He therefore combined the manner of presentation and the resources of the language in such a way that readers, in reaching for the content, were plunged into the midst of a discourse that was not chronicle, journal, history, memoir, fiction, myth, or allegory but all of them together. The prose poem can embody all of these. It allows the poet to experiment with the form of the sentence, in which the image vies with the syntax, sometimes pushing it beyond its limits. Writing of this sort makes lively reading, but is difficult to translate, and can sometimes lead to obscurity, as in the following example:

> A building gulped by the earth: seized by the hands of the
> cosmic monster lying in ambush for a world that human
> beings create on an earth commanding no view except of
> a moon and a sun and an abyss, pushing humanity into a
> bottomless pit in peering over whose edge we realize we
> didn't learn to walk, read, or use our hands except to
> reach an end that we forget, only to carry on our search
> for something that can justify this comedy and cut the
> thread connecting the beginning with the end, letting us
> imagine we are an exception to the only truth.

In some of Darwish's sentences, which as we can see here are arranged in complex rhythmic patterns that may turn back upon themselves, there is constant tension between the poetics of the image and the politics of the sentence. The image here propels the sentence toward disintegration into a syntactic arabesque of pure pattern, but is held back by the syntax itself.

It is not only a question of pattern, however. When we put this sentence back in its context, where the poet is describing a large building that had been leveled by a powerful bomb, we can comprehend that the purpose of the complexity is to reach for the sublime by expressing rage through restraint. This art is classical in its impulse and modern in its practice. In my translation I have made every effort to duplicate the poetry of the original prose, even though that may sometimes have stretched the limits of comprehensibility. As Darwish himself says in the book, "On borders, war is declared on borders." The borders here are not only those between Israel and the Arab countries, but also those of writing itself.

Although *Memory for Forgetfulness* belongs to Arabic (and now to world) literature, it is also a Palestinian text, rooted in the history, culture, and struggle of the Palestinian people. Darwish's writing here is liberationist in its impulse and represents an honest attempt to free himself and the reader from all coercive practices, be they political or aesthetic, including those whose boundaries are defined by the processes of reading and writing. As I have tried to show, the domains of the political and the aesthetic are so interwoven in Darwish's text that freedom from aesthetic coercion represents on his part a conscious act aimed at freedom from political coercion as well. I hope the translation does full justice to the original, with its playfulness, power, and depth, its music and bittersweet humor.

Memory for Forgetfulness

August, Beirut, 1982

| | | | | | | | | |

Out of one dream, another dream is born:

—*Are you well? I mean, are you alive?*

—*How did you know I was just this moment laying my head on your knee to sleep?*

—*Because you woke me up when you stirred in my belly. I knew then I was your coffin. Are you alive? Can you hear me?*

—*Does it happen much, that you are awakened from one dream by another, itself the interpretation of the dream?*

—*Here it is, happening to you and to me. Are you alive?*

—*Almost.*

—*And have the devils cast their spell on you?*

—*I don't know, but in time there's room for death.*

—*Don't die completely.*

—*I'll try not to.*

—*Don't die at all.*

—*I'll try not to.*

—*Tell me, when did it happen? I mean, when did we meet? When did we part?*

—*Thirteen years ago.*

—*Did we meet often?*

—*Twice: once in the rain, and again in the rain. The third time, we didn't meet at all. I went away and forgot you. A while*

As I point out in the Introduction, *Memory for Forgetfulness* stands on its own as a work of art, and should be read as such. Readers interested in the complexities of the political situation in Lebanon or the Arab-Israeli conflict should have no problem locating sources. Three relevant books cited below (two by David Gilmour and one by Charles Smith) have good bibliographies. I have therefore tried to keep footnotes to a minimum, mostly to provide references and contextual information where necessary. I did not think the understanding or appreciation of the work would be increased by the names of actual people for whom the author gives only initials, or those to whom he refers in other ways.

ago I remembered. I remembered I'd forgotten you. I was
dreaming.

—That also happens to me. I too was dreaming. I had your
phone number from a Swedish friend who'd met you in Beirut. I
wish you good night! Don't forget not to die. I still want you. And
when you come back to life, I want you to call me. How the time
flies! Thirteen years! No. It all happened last night. Good night!

l   l   l   l   l   l   l

Three o'clock. Daybreak riding on fire. A nightmare coming
from the sea. Roosters made of metal. Smoke. Metal preparing
a feast for metal the master, and a dawn that flares up in all the
senses before it breaks. A roaring that chases me out of bed and
throws me into this narrow hallway. I want nothing, and I hope
for nothing. I can't direct my limbs in this pandemonium. No
time for caution, and no time for time. If I only knew—if I knew
how to organize the crush of this death that keeps pouring forth.
If only I knew how to liberate the screams held back in a body
that no longer feels like mine from the sheer effort spent to save
itself in this uninterrupted chaos of shells. "Enough!" "Enough!"
I whisper, to find out if I can still do anything that will guide
me to myself and point to the abyss opening in six directions. I
can't surrender to this fate, and I can't resist it. Steel that howls,
only to have other steel bark back. The fever of metal is the song
of this dawn.

What if this inferno were to take a five-minute break, and
then come what may? Just five minutes! I almost say, "Five min-
utes only, during which I could make my one and only prepara-
tion and then ready myself for life or death." Will five minutes
be enough? Yes. Enough for me to sneak out of this narrow

hallway, open to bedroom, study, and bathroom with no water, open to the kitchen, into which for the last hour I've been ready to spring but unable to move. I'm not able to move at all.

Two hours ago I went to sleep. I plugged my ears with cotton and went to sleep after hearing the last newscast. It didn't report I was dead. That means I'm still alive. I examine the parts of my body and find them all there. *Two eyes, two ears, a long nose, ten toes below, ten fingers above, a finger in the middle.* As for the heart, it can't be seen, and I find nothing that points to it except my extraordinary ability to count my limbs and take note of a pistol lying on a bookshelf in the study. An elegant handgun—clean, sparkling, small, and empty. Along with it they also presented me with a box of bullets, which I hid I don't know where two years ago, fearing folly, fearing a stray outburst of anger, fearing a stray bullet. The conclusion is, I'm alive; or, more accurately, I exist.

No one pays heed to the wish I send up with the rising smoke: I need five minutes to place this dawn, or my share of it, on its feet and prepare to launch into this day born of howling. *Are we in August? Yes. We are in August.* The war has turned into a siege.[1] I search for news of the hour on the radio, now become a third hand, but find nobody there and no news. The radio, it seems, is asleep.

---

1. Cf. David Gilmour, *Lebanon: The Fractured Country.* (New York: St. Martin's Press, 1983):

> The siege of Lebanon's capital began a week after the invasion [launched 6 June] and lasted for two months. . . . Beirut was bombed almost constantly from 13 June to 12 August with two short intervals of about a week each at the end of June and in the middle of July. During that period it was subjected to air raids, naval bombardment, heavy artillery barrages (155 mm guns and 121 mm howitzers), and fire from tanks, mortars and rocket launchers." (p. 166)

I no longer wonder when the steely howling of the sea will stop. I live on the eighth floor of a building that might tempt any sniper, to say nothing of a fleet now transforming the sea into one of the fountainheads of hell. The north face of the building, made of glass, used to give tenants a pleasing view over the wrinkled roof of the sea. But now it offers no shield against stark slaughter. Why did I choose to live here? What a stupid question! I've lived here for the past ten years without complaining about the scandal of glass.

But how to reach the kitchen?

I want the aroma of coffee. I want nothing more than the aroma of coffee. And I want nothing more from the passing days than the aroma of coffee. The aroma of coffee so I can hold myself together, stand on my feet, and be transformed from something that crawls, into a human being. The aroma of coffee so I can stand my share of this dawn up on its feet. So that we can go together, this day and I, down into the street in search of another place.

How can I diffuse the aroma of coffee into my cells, while shells from the sea rain down on the sea-facing kitchen, spreading the stink of gunpowder and the taste of nothingness? I measure the period between two shells. One second. One second: shorter than the time between breathing in and breathing out, between two heartbeats. One second is not long enough for me to stand before the stove by the glass facade that overlooks the sea. One second is not long enough to open the water bottle or pour the water into the coffee pot. One second is not long enough to light a match. But one second is long enough for me to burn.

I switch off the radio, no longer wondering if the wall of

this narrow hallway will actually protect me from the rain of rockets. What matters is that a wall be there to veil air fusing into metal, seeking human flesh, making a direct hit, choking it, or scattering shrapnel. In such cases a mere dark curtain is enough to provide an imaginary shield of safety. For death is to see death.

I want the aroma of coffee. I need five minutes. I want a five-minute truce for the sake of coffee. I have no personal wish other than to make a cup of coffee. With this madness I define my task and my aim. All my senses are on their mark, ready at the call to propel my thirst in the direction of the one and only goal: coffee.

Coffee, for an addict like me, is the key to the day.

And coffee, for one who knows it as I do, means making it with your own hands and not having it come to you on a tray, because the bringer of the tray is also the bearer of talk, and the first coffee, the virgin of the silent morning, is spoiled by the first words. Dawn, my dawn, is antithetical to chatter. The aroma of coffee can absorb sounds and will go rancid, even if these sounds are nothing more than a gentle "Good morning!"

Coffee is the morning silence, early and unhurried, the only silence in which you can be at peace with self and things, cre-ative, standing alone with some water that you reach for in lazy solitude and pour into a small copper pot with a mysterious shine—yellow turning to brown—that you place over a low fire. *Oh, that it were a wood fire!*

Stand back from the fire a little and observe a street that has been rising to search for its bread ever since the ape disentangled himself from the trees and walked on two feet. A street borne along on carts loaded with fruits and vegetables, and vendors'

cries notable for faint praise that turns produce into a mere at-
tribute of price. Stand back a little and breathe air sent by the
cool night. Then return to your low fire—*If only it were a wood
fire!*—and watch with love and patience the contact between the
two elements, fire colored green and blue and water roiling and
breathing out tiny white granules that turn into a fine film and
grow. Slowly they expand, then quickly swell into bubbles that
grow bigger and bigger, and break. Swelling and breaking,
they're thirsty and ready to swallow two spoonfuls of coarse
sugar, which no sooner penetrates than the bubbles calm down
to a quiet hiss, only to sizzle again in a cry for a substance that
is none other than the coffee itself—a flashy rooster of aroma
and Eastern masculinity.

Remove the pot from the low fire to carry on the dialogue
of a hand, free of the smell of tobacco and ink, with its first crea-
tion, which as of this moment will determine the flavor of your
day and the arc of your fortune: whether you're to work or avoid
contact with anyone for the day. What emerges from this first
motion and its rhythm, from what shakes it out of a world of
sleep rising from the previous day, and from whatever mystery it
will uncover in you, will form the identity of your new day.

Because coffee, the first cup of coffee, is the mirror of the
hand. And the hand that makes the coffee reveals the person
that stirs it. Therefore, coffee is the public reading of the open
book of the soul. And it is the enchantress that reveals whatever
secrets the day will bring.

| | | | | | | |

The dawn made of lead is still advancing from the direction of
the sea, riding on sounds I haven't heard before. The sea has

been entirely packed into stray shells. It is changing its marine nature and turning into metal. Does death have all these names? We said we'd leave. Why then does this red-black-gray rain keep pouring over those leaving or staying, be they people, trees, or stones? We said we'd leave. "By sea?" they asked. "By sea," we answered. Why then are they arming the foam and waves with this heavy artillery? Is it to hasten our steps to the sea? But first they must break the siege of the sea. They must clear the last path for the last thread of our blood. But that they won't do, so we won't be leaving. I'll go ahead then and make the coffee.

| | | | | | |

The neighborhood birds are awake at six in the morning. They've kept the tradition of neutral song ever since they found themselves alone with the first glimmer of light. For whom do they sing in the crush of these rockets? They sing to heal their nature of a night that has passed. They sing for themselves, not for us. Did we realize that before? The birds clear their own space in the smoke of the burning city, and the zigzagging arrows of sound wrap themselves around the shells and point to an earth safe under the sky. It is for the killer to kill, the fighter to fight, and the bird to sing. As for me, I halt my quest for figurative language. I bring my search for meaning to a complete stop because the essence of war is to degrade symbols and bring human relations, space, time, and the elements back to a state of nature, making us rejoice over water gushing on the road from a broken pipe.

Water under these conditions comes to us like a miracle. Who says water has no color, flavor, or smell? Water does have a color that reveals itself in the unfolding of thirst. Water has the color of bird sounds, that of sparrows in particular—birds that pay no heed to this war approaching from the sea, so long as their space is safe. And water has the flavor of water, and a fragrance that is the scent of the afternoon breeze blown from a field with full ears of wheat waving in a luminous expanse strewn like the flickering spots of light left by the wings of a small sparrow fluttering low. Not everything that flies is an airplane. (Perhaps one of the worst Arabic words is *Ta:'irah*—airplane—which is the feminine form of *Ta:'ir*—bird.) The birds carry on with their song, insistent in the midst of the naval artillery's roar. Who said water has no flavor, color, or smell, and that this jet is the feminine form of this bird?

But suddenly the birds are quiet. They stop their chatter and routine soaring in the dawn air when the storm of flying metal starts to blow. Are they quiet because of its steely roar, or from the incongruity of name and form? Two wings of steel and silver versus two made of feathers. A nose of wiring and steel against a beak made of song. A cargo of rockets against a grain of wheat and a straw. Their skies no longer safe, the birds stop singing and pay heed to the war.

| | | | | | | |

The sky sinks like a sagging concrete roof. The sea approaches, changing into dry land. Sky and sea are one substance, making it hard to breathe. I switch on the radio. Nothing. Time has frozen. It sits on me, choking me. The jets pass between my fingers. They pierce my lungs. How can I reach the aroma of coffee? Am I to shrivel up and die without the aroma of coffee? *I don't want. I don't want.* Where's my will?

It stopped there, on the other side of the street, the day we raised the call against the legend advancing on us from the south. The day human flesh clenched the muscles of its spirit and cried, "They shall not pass, and we will not leave!" Flesh engaged against metal: it won against the difficult arithemtic, and the conquerors were halted by the walls. There will be time to bury the dead. There will be time for weaponry. And there will be time to pass the time as we please, that this heroism may go on. Because now we are the masters of time.

Bread sprang from the soil and water gushed from the rocks. Their rockets dug wells for us, and the language of their killing tempted us to sing, "We will not leave!" We saw our faces on foreign screens boiling with great promise and breaking through the siege with unwavering victory signs. From now on we have nothing to lose, so long as Beirut is here and we're here in Beirut as names for a different homeland, where meanings will find their words again in the midst of this sea and on the edge of this desert. For here, where we are, is the tent for wandering meanings and words gone astray and the orphaned light, scattered and banished from the center.

But do they realize, these youths armed to the teeth with a creative ignorance of the balance of forces and with the opening words of old songs, with hand grenades and burning beer bottles, with the desires of girls in air-raid shelters and pieces of torn identities, with a clear wish to take vengeance on prudent parents and with what they do not know of the sport of active death; armed with a rage for release from the senility of the Idea—do they realize that with their wounds and inventive recklessness they are correcting the ink of a language that (from the siege of Acre in the Middle Ages to the present siege of Beirut whose aim is revenge for all medieval history) has driven the whole area east of the Mediterranean toward a West that has wanted nothing more from slavery than to make enslavement easier?[2]

And when they set about putting the siege under siege, did they know that in bringing the actual out of the marvelous into the ordinary they were supplanting the legend and revealing to the misguided Prophet of Doom the secrets of a heroism woven by the movement from the self-evident to the self-evident? As if a man were to be tested on being male, and a woman on being female; as if dignity had the power to choose between self-defense and suicide; or as if a lone knight had a choice other than single-handedly to cleave this insolent space and clear a path to the secret motive within him, rather than accept that his personal valor and his moral and physical heroism must await the return of official chivalry. As if a handful of human beings were to rebel against the order of things so that this people, whose birth was tempered with stubborn fire, should not be made equal to a flock of sheep herded over the fence of complicity by the Shepherds of Oppression in collusion with the Guardian of the Legend.[3]

They shall not pass as long as there's life in our bodies. Let them pass, then, if they can pass at all, over whatever corpses the spirit may spit out.

---

2. The "youths armed to the teeth" (known as the "RPG [rocket-propelled grenade] kids") are Palestinian children born in the refugee camps of Lebanon. Alongside regular Palestinian and Lebanese fighters, they showed great heroism in resisting the Israeli invasion.

3. The "legend" is a reference to the Israeli army, and the "Prophet of Doom" is most likely a reference to Ariel Sharon, the Israeli minister of defense, who launched the invasion of Lebanon in 1982. The "Shepherds of Oppression" are the Arab leaders, and the "Guardian of the Legend," as we find out later in the text, is a reference to Menachem Begin, the Israeli prime minister at the time.

And where is my will?

It stopped over there, on the other side of the collective voice. But now, I want nothing more than the aroma of coffee. Now I feel shame. I feel shamed by my fear, and by those defending the scent of the distant homeland—that fragrance they've never smelled because they weren't born on her soil. She bore them, but they were born away from her. Yet they studied her constantly, without fatigue or boredom; and from overpowering memory and constant pursuit, they learned what it means to belong to her.

"You're aliens here," they say to them *there.*

"You're aliens here," they say to them *here.*[4]

And between *here* and *there* they stretched their bodies like a vibrating bow until death celebrated itself through them. Their parents were driven out of *there* to become guests *here,* temporary guests, to clear civilians from the battlegrounds of the homeland and to allow the regular armies to purge Arab land and honor of shame and disgrace. As the old lyric had it: "Brother, the oppressors have all limits dared to break / To battle then, of ourselves an offering to make . . . / Of a sudden upon them with death we came / In vain their fight, and nothing they became."[5] And as those lyrics were chasing out the remnants of the invaders, liberating the country line by line, these

4. Recurring throughout, "there" and "here" represent two major poles of experience in the text. Literally, they are references to Palestine (there) and Lebanon (here).

5. After the loss of Palestine in 1948, this lyric was made famous by the Egyptian singer Muhammad Abd al-Wahhab (to whom there is another reference later in the text). To Darwish, an innovative and experimental poet, the lyric represents the decadent use of the *qaSi:da*—the classical form of Arabic verse. The reference in the sentence following the lyric to "liberating the country line by line" is extremely bitter and ironic, since the country was actually lost

youths were being born here, any old way—without a cradle, perhaps on a straw mat or banana leaves, or in bamboo baskets—with no joy or feasting, no birth certificate or name registration. They were a burden to their families and tent neighbors. In short, their births were surplus. They had no identity.

And in the end what happened, happened. The regular armies retreated, and these youths were still being born without a reason, growing up for no reason, remembering for no reason, and being put under siege for no reason. All of them know the story—a story very much like that of a cosmic traffic accident or a natural catastrophe. But they also read a great deal in the books of their bodies and their shacks. They read their segregation, and the Arab-nationalist speeches. They read the publications of UNRWA, and the whips of the police.[6] Yet they went on growing up and going beyond the limits of the refugee camp and the detention center.

And they read the history of forts and citadels conquerors used as signatures to keep their names alive in lands not theirs and to forge the identity of rocks and oranges, for example. Is history not bribable? And why, then, would many places—lakes, mountains, cities—bear the names of military leaders but that

---

while that kind of poetry was still being written. The lyric's content demonstrates another form of decadence for a poet who, as we see from this book, has an overriding concern with language; it shows the vacuity of pre-1967 Arab political discourse in general and discourse about Israel in particular. The Arab defeat in 1967 (a watershed year in modern Arab history and a major theme in the book) opened the eyes of many intellectuals to the need for renewal on all fronts.

6. UNRWA, the United Nations Relief and Works Agency, was created in 1950 to take care of Palestinians living in the refugee camps in the Arab countries when "it became clear no resolution of the refugee question was likely." Charles C. Smith, *Palestine and the Arab-Israeli Conflict* (New York: St. Martin's Press, 1992), p. 154.

they had mouthed an impression when they first beheld them, and their words became the names still used today? "Oh, rid!" (How beautiful!) That's what a Roman general cried out when he first saw that lake in Macedonia, and his surprise became its name. Add to this the hundreds of names we use to refer to places previously singled out by some conqueror, where it has since become difficult to disentangle the identity from the defeat. Forts and citadels that are no more than attempts to protect a name that does not trust time to preserve it from oblivion. Anti-forgetfulness wars; anti-oblivion stones. No one wants to forget. More accurately, no one wants to be forgotten. Or, more peacefully, people bring children into the world to carry their name, or to bear for them the weight of the name and its glory. It has had a long history, this double operation of searching for a place or a time on which to put a signature and untie the knot of the name facing the long caravans of oblivion.

Why then should those whom the waves of forgetfulness have cast upon the shores of Beirut be expected to go against nature? Why should so much amnesia be expected of them? And who can construct for them a new memory with no content other than the broken shadow of a distant life in a shack made of sheet metal?

Is there enough forgetfulness for them to forget?

And who is going to help them forget in the midst of this anguish, which never stops reminding them of their alienation from place and society? Who will accept them as citizens? Who will protect them against the whips of discrimination and pursuit: "You don't belong here!"

They present for inspection an identity, which, shown at borders, sounds an alarm so that contagious diseases may be kept in check, and at the same time they note how expertly this very identity is used to uplift Arab-nationalist spirit. These forgotten ones, disconnected from the social fabric, these outcasts, deprived of work and equal rights, are at the same time expected to applaud their oppression because it provides them with the blessings of memory. Thus he who's expected to forget he's human is forced to accept the exclusion from human rights that will train him for freedom from the disease of forgetting the homeland. He has to catch tuberculosis not to forget he has lungs, and he must sleep in open country not to forget he has another sky. He has to work as a servant not to forget he has a national duty, and he must be denied the privilege of settling down so that he won't forget Palestine. In short, he must remain the Other to his Arab brothers because he is pledged to liberation.

Fine, fine. He knows his duty: *my identity—my gun.* Why then do they level against him countless accusations: making trouble, violating the rules of hospitality, creating problems, and spreading the contagion of arms? When he holds his peace, his soul is taken out to the stray dogs; and when he moves toward the homeland, his body is dragged out to the dogs. The intellectuals, capable of trying on the latest models in theory, have convinced him he's the only alternative to the status quo; yet when the status quo pounces on him, they demand self-criticism because he has gone too far in his patriotism: he has gone so far as to put himself beyond the fold of the status quo. *Conditions are not ripe. Conditions are not yet ripe. He has to wait.* What must he do? Chatter his life away in the coffee shops of Beirut? He had already prattled so long he was told Beirut had corrupted him.

Society ladies, armed with automatic weapons, amid the tinkle of their jewelry give speeches at parties organized for the defense of the national origins of *mujaddara*. Yet when he feels embarrassed by this and says something to the effect that the homeland is not a dish of rice and lentils, and when he takes up arms for use outside, on the border, they say, "This is overstepping the bounds." And when he uses these arms to defend himself inside, against the local agents of Zionism, they say, "This is interference in our communal affairs." What's to be done then? What can he do to end the process of self-criticism, other than apologize for an existence which has not yet come into being? *You are not going there, and you don't belong here.* Between these two negations this generation was born defending the spirit's bodily vessel, onto which they fasten the fragrance of the country they've never known. They've read what they've read, and they've seen what they've seen, and they don't believe defeat is inevitable. So they set out on the trail of that fragrance.

| | | | | | |

They shame me, without my knowing I'm ashamed in front of them. The obscure heaps up on the obscure, rubs against itself, and ignites into clarity. Conquerors can do anything. They can aim sea, sky, and earth at me, but they cannot root the aroma of coffee out of me. I shall make my coffee now. I will drink the coffee now. Right now, I will be sated with the aroma of coffee, that I may at least distinguish myself from a sheep and live one more day, or die, with the aroma of coffee all around me.

Move the pot away from the low fire, that the hand may undertake its first creation of the day. Pay no heed to rockets, shells, or jets. This is what I want. To possess my dawn, I'll diffuse the aroma of coffee. Don't look at the mountain spitting masses of fire in the direction of your hand. But alas, you can't forget that over there, in Ashrafiya, they're dancing in ecstasy. Yesterday's papers showed the carnation ladies throwing themselves at the invaders' tanks, their bosoms and thighs bare in summer nakedness and pleasure, ready to receive the saviors:

Kiss me on the lips, Shlomo! O kiss me on the lips! What's your name, my love, so I can call you by your name, my darling? Shlomo, my heart's been passionately longing for you. Come in, Shlomo, come into my house, slowly, slowly, or all at once so I can feel your strength. How I love strength, my darling! And shell them, my love, slaughter them! Kill them with all the passion waiting in us. May the Blessed Lady of Lebanon protect you, Mr. Shlomo! Shell them, sweetheart, while I prepare a glass of arak and your lunch. In how many hours will you finish them off, my darling? How many hours will it take? But the operation has gone on too long, Shlomo, too long! Why are you so slow, my love? Two months! Why haven't you been advancing? And Shlomo, your body odors are rank. Never mind! That's no doubt due to the heat and the sweat. I'll wash you in jasmine water, my love. But why are you pissing in the street? Do you speak French? No? Where were you born? In Ta'ez? Where's this Ta'ez? In Yemen? No matter. No matter. I thought you were different. It doesn't matter, Shlomo. Just shell over there for my sake, over there![7]

Gently place one spoonful of the ground coffee, electrified with the aroma of cardamom, on the rippling surface of the hot water, then stir slowly, first clockwise, then up and down. Add

7. This passage is a bitter reference to the welcome given the Israeli army in the early days of the invasion in Ashrafiya, the stronghold of the Phalangist militia, by the members of the Maronite community.

the second spoonful and stir up and down, then counterclockwise. Now add the third. Between spoonfuls, take the pot away from the fire and bring it back. For the final touch, dip the spoon in the melting powder, fill and raise it a little over the pot, then let it drop back. Repeat this several times until the water boils again and a small mass of the blond coffee remains on the surface, rippling and ready to sink. Don't let it sink. Turn off the heat, and pay no heed to the rockets. Take the coffee to the narrow corridor and pour it lovingly and with a sure hand into a little white cup: dark-colored cups spoil the freedom of the coffee. Observe the paths of the steam and the tent of rising aroma. Now light your first cigarette, made for this cup of coffee, the cigarette with the flavor of existence itself, unequaled by the taste of any other except that which follows love, as the woman smokes away the last sweat and the fading voice.

Now I am born. My veins are saturated with their stimulant drugs, in contact with the springs of their life, caffeine and nicotine, and the ritual of their coming together as created by my hand. "How can a hand write," I ask myself, "if it doesn't know how to be creative in making coffee!" How often have the heart specialists said, while smoking, "Don't smoke or drink coffee!" And how I've joked with them, "A donkey doesn't smoke or drink coffee. And it doesn't write."

I know my coffee, my mother's coffee, and the coffee of my friends. I can tell them from afar and I know the differences among them. No coffee is like another, and my defense of coffee is a plea for difference itself. There's no flavor we might label "the flavor of coffee" because coffee is not a concept, or even a single substance. And it's not an absolute. Everyone's coffee is special, so special that I can tell one's taste and elegance of spirit by the flavor of the coffee. Coffee with the flavor of coriander means the woman's kitchen is not organized. Coffee with the flavor of carob juice means the host is stingy. Coffee with the aroma of perfume means the lady is too concerned with appearances. Coffee that feels like moss in the mouth means its maker is an infantile leftist. Coffee that tastes stale from too much turning over in the hot water means its maker is an extreme rightist. And coffee with the overwhelming flavor of cardamom means the lady is newly rich.

No coffee is like another. Every house has its coffee, and every hand too, because no soul is like another. I can tell coffee from far away: it moves in a straight line at first, then zigzags, winds, bends, sighs, and turns on flat, rocky surfaces and slopes; it wraps itself around an oak, then loosens and drops into a wadi, looks back, and melts with longing to go up the mountain. It does go up the mountain as it disperses in the gossamer of a shepherd's pipe taking it back to its first home.

The aroma of coffee is a return to and a bringing back of first things because it is the offspring of the primordial. It's a journey, begun thousands of years ago, that still goes on. Coffee is a place. Coffee is pores that let the inside seep through to the outside. A separation that unites what can't be united except through its aroma. Coffee is not for weaning. On the contrary, coffee is a breast that nourishes men deeply. A morning born of a bitter taste. The milk of manhood. Coffee is geography.

| | | | | | |

Who is that rising out of my dream?

Did she really speak with me before dawn, or was I delirious, dreaming while waking?

We met only twice. The first time, she learned my name; and the second, I learned hers. The third time, we didn't meet at all. Why then is she calling me now, out of a dream in which I was sleeping on her knee? The first time, I didn't say to her, "I love you." And the second, she didn't say to me, "I love you." And we never drank coffee together.

| | | | | | |

I got used to counting the number of weevils in the dish of lentil soup, our daily fare in prison. And I got used to overcoming my disgust, because appetite is flexible, and hunger is stronger than appetite. But I never did get used to the absence of my morning coffee and having to take washed-out tea instead. Was that why I never adapted to prison life? A friend asked after my first release from prison, "Did you have a good time?" "No," I answered, "because they didn't offer coffee." "Shocking!" she exclaimed, "though I don't drink coffee." "I don't know many women who are obsessed with coffee in the morning," I answered. "Men open their day with coffee; women prefer makeup."

That was not what grieved me, though. One morning a fellow prisoner managed to bring me a cup of coffee. I fell upon it with lust but gave myself time to contemplate it, which only moved another prisoner to cast longing glances in the direction of the cup. I ignored him, to be one with my possession. I ignored him and sipped the coffee with a sadistic pleasure that later gave rise to feelings of guilt.

That was twenty years ago, yet that imploring look still haunts me, always urging me to reexamine myself and correct my behavior, because giving and sharing in prison are the very measure of generosity. I never could get rid of that guilt despite my showering him with cigarette halves in an attempt to buy back my psychological balance. What selfishness! I had deprived a fellow prisoner of half a cup of coffee, which motivated the fates to punish me. A week later my mother came to visit, bringing with her a pot full of coffee, but the guard poured it on the grass.

| | | | | | | |

Coffee should not be drunk in a hurry. It is the sister of time, and should be sipped slowly, slowly. Coffee is the sound of taste, a sound for the aroma. It is a meditation and a plunge into memories and the soul. And coffee is a habit which, along with the cigarette, must be joined with another habit—the newspaper.

Where is the newspaper? It's six o'clock in the morning, and I'm in hell itself. But the news is that which is read, not heard. And before it is recorded, the event is not exactly an event. I know a researcher in Israeli affairs who kept denying the "rumor" that Beirut was under siege simply because what he read was not the truth unless it was written in Hebrew. And since Israeli newspapers had not yet reached him, he wouldn't acknowledge that Beirut was under siege. But this is not a madness I suffer from. For me, the morning paper is an addiction. Where is the newspaper?

The hysteria of the jets is rising. The sky has gone crazy. Utterly wild. This dawn is a warning that today will be the last day of creation. Where are they going to strike next? Where are they not going to strike? Is the area around the airport big enough to absorb all these shells, capable of murdering the sea itself? I turn on the radio and am forced to listen to happy commercials: "Merit cigarettes—more aroma, less nicotine!" "Citizen watches—for the correct time!" "Come to Marlboro, come to where the pleasure is!" "Health mineral water—health from a high mountain!" But where is the water? Increasing coyness from the women announcers on Radio Monte Carlo, who sound as if they've just emerged from taking a bath or from an exciting bedroom: "Intensive bombardment of Beirut." *Intensive bombardment of Beirut!* Is this aired as an ordinary news item about an ordinary day in an ordinary war in an ordinary newscast? I move the dial to the BBC. Deadly lukewarm voices of announcers smoking pipes within hearing of the listeners. Voices broadcast over shortwave and magnified to a medium wave that transforms them into repulsive vocal caricatures: "Our correspondent says it would appear to cautious observers that what appears of what is gradually becoming clearer when the spokesman is enabled except for the difficulty in getting in touch with the events, which would perhaps indicate that both warring parties are no doubt trying especially not to mention a certain ambiguity which may reveal fighter planes with unknown pilots circling over if we want to be accurate for it might confirm that some people are now appearing in beautiful clothes." A formal Arabic with correct information, ending with a song by Muhammad Abd al-Wahhab in colloquial Arabic with the correct emotion: "Either come see me, or tell me where to meet you / Or else tell me where to go, to leave you alone."

Identically monotonous voices. Sand describing sea. Eloquent voices beyond reproach, describing death as they would the weather, and not as they would a horse or motorcycle race. What am I searching for? I open the door several times, but find no newspaper. Why am I looking for the paper when buildings are falling in all directions? Is that not writing enough?

That's not quite right. The one looking for a paper in the midst of this hell is running from a solitary to a collective death. He's looking for a pair of human eyes, for a shared silence or reciprocal talk. He's looking for some kind of participation in this death, for a witness who can give evidence, for a gravestone over a corpse, for the bearer of news about the fall of a horse, for a language of speech and silence, and for a less boring wait for certain death. For what this steel and these iron beasts are screaming is that no one will be left in peace, and no one will count our dead.

I'm lying to myself: I have no need to search for a description of my surroundings or my leaky interiors. The truth of the matter is that I am terrified of falling among the ruins, prey to a moaning no one can hear. And that is painful. Painful to the extent of my feeling the pain as if the event had actually happened. I'm now there, in the rubble. I feel the pain of the animal crushed inside me. I cry out in pain but no one hears me. This is a phantom pain, coming from an opposite direction—out of what might happen. Some of those hit in the leg continue to feel pain there for several years after amputation. They reach out to feel the pain in a place where there is no longer a limb. This phantom, imaginary pain may pursue them to the end of their days. As for me, I feel the pain of an injury that hasn't happened. My legs have been crushed under the rubble.

These are my forebodings. Perhaps it won't be a rocket that'll kill me in a flash, without my being aware. Perhaps a wall will slowly, slowly fall on me, and my suffering will be endless, with no one to hear my cries for help. It may crush my leg, my arm, or my skull. Or it may sit over my chest, and I'll stay alive for several days in which no one will have the time to search for the remains of another being. Perhaps splinters from my glasses will lodge in my eyes and blind me. My side may be pierced by a metal rod, or I may be forgotten in the crush of mangled flesh left behind in the rubble.

But why am I so concerned with what will happen to my corpse and where it will end up? I don't know. I want a well-organized funeral, in which they'll put my body whole, not mangled, in a wooden coffin wrapped in a flag with the four colors clearly visible (even if their names come from a line of poetry whose sounds don't signify their meanings), carried on the shoulders of my friends and those of my friends who are my enemies.[8]

And I want wreaths of red and yellow roses. I don't want the cheap pink color, and I don't want violets, because they spread the smell of death. And I want a radio announcer who's not a chatterer, whose voice is not too throaty, and who can put on a convincing show of sadness. Between tapes carrying my words, I want him to make little speeches. I want a calm, orderly funeral; and I want it big, that leave-taking, unlike meeting, may be beautiful. How good is the fortune of the recently dead on the first day of mourning, when the mourners compete in praise of them! They're knights for one day, loved for a day, and innocent for that day. No slander, no curses, and no envy. It'll be

---

8. The colors of the Palestinian flag are white, black, green, and red. The line of poetry mentioned in the text is "White are our deeds, black our battles; green are our pastures, and red our swords." Darwish's description of it as a line "whose sounds don't signify their meanings" is yet another way of referring to the disparity between form and content alluded to in note 5.

even better for me, because I've no wife or children. That'll save friends the effort of having to put on the long, sad act that doesn't end until the widow feels compassion for the mourner. It'll also save the children the indignity of having to stand at the doors of institutions run by tribal bureaucracies. It's good I'm alone, alone, alone. For that reason my funeral will be free of charge, no one having to keep an account of reciprocal courtesy, so that after the funeral those who walked in the procession can go back to their daily affairs. I want a funeral with an elegant coffin, from which I can peep out over the mourners, just as the playwright Tawfiq al-Hakim wanted to do. I want to sneak a look at how they stand, walk, and sigh and how they convert their spittle into tears. I also want to eavesdrop on their mocking comments: "He was a womanizer." "He was a dandy in his choice of clothes." "The rugs in his house are so plush you sink into them up to your knees." "He had a palace on the French Riviera, a villa in Spain, and a secret bank account in Zurich. And he kept a private plane, secretly, and five luxury cars in a garage in Beirut." "We don't know if he had a yacht in Greece, but he had enough sea shells in his house to build a whole refugee camp." "He used to lie to women." "The poet is dead, and his poetry with him. What's left of him? His role is finished, and we're done with his legend. He took his poetry with him and disappeared. Anyway, his nose was long, and his tongue." I'll hear even harsher stuff than this, once the imagination has been let loose. I'll smile in my coffin and try to say, "Enough!" I'll try to come back to life, but I won't be able.

| | | | | |

But to die here—no! I don't want to die under the rubble. I'll pretend I'm going down to the street to look for a newspaper. Fear is shameful in the midst of this fever of heroism erupting from the people—from those on the front line whose names we don't know, as well as the simple souls who have chosen to stay in Beirut, to devote their days to the search for enough water to fill a twenty-liter can in this downpour of bombs, to extend the moment of resistance and steadfastness into history, and to pay the price with their flesh in the battle against exploding metal. Heroism is here in this very part of divided Beirut in this burning summer. It is West Beirut. He who dies here does not die by chance. Rather he who lives, lives by chance, because not one span of earth has been spared the rockets and not one spot where you can take a step has been saved from an explosion. But I don't want to die under the rubble. I want to die in the open street.

Suddenly, worms, made famous in a certain novel, spread before me. Worms arranging themselves in rigid order into rows according to color and type to consume a corpse, stripping flesh off bone in a few minutes. Just one raid. Two raids, and nothing's left except the skeleton. Worms that come from nowhere, from the earth, from the corpse itself. The corpse consumes itself by means of a well-organized army rising from within it in moments. Surely, it's a picture that empties a man of heroism and flesh, thrusting him into the nakedness of absurd destiny, into absolute absurdity, into total nothingness; a picture that peels the song from the praise of death and from the escape into flight. Was it to overcome the ugliness of this fact that the human imagination—the inhabitant of the corpse—opened a space to save the spirit from this nothingness? Is this the solution proposed by religion and poetry? Perhaps. Perhaps.

| | | | | | |

Because I had known Samir from childhood, I didn't go to the hospital when he was in a coma. The jets had mangled his legs and one of his arms, had ripped open his belly and gouged out his eyes as he was evacuating the wounded from the square of the Sports City. What was left of him? I mean, what was left of the looks that had lit fires under the skirts of girls? We were schoolmates in Kufur Yasif. He never came to class much. He was absentminded and absent, and preferred going to the sea and chasing birds to reading his books. He never took part in student pranks. He was as handsome as the biblical Joseph, and shy without being pious. Clear blue eyes from the sea at Acre and from his beautiful, tyrannical mother. Curly hair, the color of chestnuts, and a broad forehead commanding a view above us. He was very remote, and physically strong. We never knew why he decided to leave school, family, and homeland behind until he set off the June War. At least that was what the Israeli papers had claimed in huge headlines: "Arrest of a Fedayee Infiltrating the Border to Blow Up Haifa." It was the eve of the June War of 1967, and Israeli propaganda was bent on preparing the ground for the war. Since he had never shared our activism before, we didn't believe Samir was a fedayee until his tall, manacled body looked out on us from the newspaper. His father, my cousin, told me how the police had made him listen through the

wall to Samir's moans under continuous torture. A pack of
wolves preying on a captive gazelle. He was completely de-
stroyed as he listened to the sounds of slow death emerging from
the body of his pampered son, elegant and handsome, raised in
comfort and plenty. But his mother, a woman of striking beauty,
was able to calm her nerves and preserve her psychological bal-
ance through motherly pride, awakened by the perception that
her son was now a man who had challenged a state that had
defeated other states. She thus turned her sadness into pride.

They sentenced Samir to life. In prison he acted the collabo-
rator, holding up under the gibes of his fellow fedayeen, until he
put his plan into action. He worked in the prison kitchen, where
he could get hold of the sharp tools he needed, and for months
he worked to cut through the iron bars of his cell until zero
hour arrived and he was able to free a few of his fellow prisoners.
He insisted on being the last to escape, but by then the guards
had caught on to the operation and they pulled him back from
the bars of the window. Again they sentenced him to life. After
a third try, they gave him a third life sentence. Thus, he would
have had to live three lifetimes to gain his freedom.

After a prisoner exchange Samir finally emerged into the
light of the great Arab homeland but could not believe the dif-
ference between the Idea and its expression. He couldn't accept
the contradiction between the dream and its vehicle and took
comfort in the prisoner's traditional comparison of the outside,
and its apparent freedom, with the inside, and its imagined free-
dom, a freedom that springs from firm convictions, peace of
mind, and the link to the world outside, held as a model. We've
gotten used to the complaints of those who come out of their

inner freedom into our distorted freedom, just as we've grown accustomed to their disappointment with all that distorts their idea of us and their image of what it's like on the outside.

When I saw him in Damascus twenty years later, Samir said, "Can this really be the way it is? It wasn't for this that I went in, and not for this that I came out!" But he had enough loyalty to the ties holding the Organization and the ideal together to prevent him from taking disillusionment to an extreme by advocating that the vehicle be replaced by something more harmonious and better balanced. He was highly disappointed with the national institutions, but very attached to them. "A man like me," he said, "can't just change his skin, not because the Organization intimidates him, but out of fear that one of the elements holding it in balance might collapse. Let me then consider myself a servant to the idea of Palestine and its people, whether I belong to this faction or that, without getting drawn into factional struggles or the deceit that follows from the choice by some of them (and they don't even represent me) of this or that Arab regime for a master."

He set himself apart, shielding himself under the wing of absolutes. He was afraid that any change in his cadre might discredit the truth of its history and the warmth of its spirit of sacrifice, because dissent, in the absence of values that an actual society and a homeland could bring into being, was likely to raise the doubts and suspicions that prevail in wars of words not constrained by morality or patriotism. This sort of "national dialogue" has never given birth to anything but assassination, and none of us is free from having leveled accusations.

Samir stayed in Beirut, only to continue asking his cutting questions about freedom in prison and prison in a freedom open to corruption and the suspension of discipline where, for example, a spokesman for this "freedom" could bring down a building on its inhabitants just to settle accounts with another member of the faction, without losing his position or his right loudly to represent this or that Arab regime in the leadership. Perhaps a judgment the Palestinian revolution deserves is that it has lacked a tradition of trying those of its leaders who have committed flagrant crimes. So far, the only trials have been those for "crimes against morality," committed by young future martyrs in their search for passing pleasure in a marijuana cigarette or the arms of a seductive woman before they are turned into convenient excuses for rousing speeches. It was difficult for Samir, and others like him who had come out of Israeli prisons, to understand how representatives of Arab secret services could become leaders in the national movement on the pretext that the Revolution must keep a "balance" in dealing with other nations. Are we the Arab League? He was never able to get used to these confused traditions because he never matured, never reached the degree of "realism" gained only through knowledge of the great strides Palestinian political discourse has taken in its complex relations with the Arab base and the Arab summit. When this discourse found itself prisoner rather than pampered son, once the question of democracy was severed from that of Arab nationalism, each going in an opposite direction, the result was that our "national unity" drew one of its constitutive elements from the solidarity of Arab governments, not with the Organization but within it.

Yet Samir, who was tortured with questions about freedom in prison and prison in freedom, plunged headlong into a wave of general indulgence that swept us all to the shores of fatalism.

And because I had known him since childhood, I didn't go to visit him at Barbir Hospital. "You won't recognize him," they said. "And if you love him," they added, "pray for him to die, because death is his only release. He's in a coma. He has gone into death, alive."

They had not released him from prison after all. They overtook him in Beirut, exchanging a life sentence in prison for execution by jet. Samir is dead. The basil plant of the family is dead.

| | | | | | |

I don't want to die disfigured under the rubble. I want to be hit in the middle of the street by a shell, suddenly. I want to burn completely, to turn into charcoal, so that not even those worms in the novel can do their eternal duty on me: worms don't eat charcoal. I'll therefore say to myself I'm looking for a newspaper, to justify my walking in a street empty even of cats and dogs. I'll pay no heed to what's happening outside the window—shells, rockets, ships, jets, artillery—all blowing my way like a raging wind, falling like rain, shaking the place like an earthquake. Human will can't do anything against these; they're a fate that can't be turned back. All the unimaginably evil inventions human creativity has ever come up with and all the advances technology has achieved—their efficacy is now being tested on our bodies. Will this be the longest day in history? No one is washing the dead. Let the dead then wash themselves—I mean with blood flowing more freely than water. I hoard my treasure of water and use each drop with extreme care. Every drop has a role. I almost have to measure water in drops. Five hundred for washing the hair. Two thousand for the body. One hundred for the mouth. One hundred for shaving. Twenty for each ear. Fifty for each armpit. And . . . And . . . For every drop there's a corresponding part of the body.

What is water? Who says it has no color, flavor, or odor? What is water? Chemically, it's H_2O. But is it only that? What, then, is the fragrance that opens out the skin, to bring us to a feast there, in the vastness of the body and its quarters, until we almost take on the nature of butterflies? Water is the joy of the senses and the air that surrounds them. Water is that very air, distilled, tangible, perceptible, saturated with light. For this reason, prophets have urged their people to love water: "We made from water every living thing."[9] I remember Ibn Fadlan's *Epistle* and feel nauseated by that one vessel of water used to wash a whole army.[10] Our water has been cut by those acting on behalf of leftover Crusaders, yet Saladin used to send ice and fruits to

9. The Prophets, Qur'an 21:30.

10. Ibn Fadlan's *Epistle* (Risa:lat Ibn FaDla:n) is the record of a journey into Russia, undertaken in A.D. 921 (A.H. 309) on behalf of the Abbasid Caliph al-Muqtadir billa:h by a four-member delegation headed by Ahmad Ibn Fadlan, who kept a careful record of the peoples and tribes he visited. As far as I can determine, the reference to water used again and again for washing occurs in his description of a group he calls "the Russians," but there is no reference to an army in the text. In describing the customs of these people, Ibn Fadlan says that from ten to twenty people lived in one house, and that

> they must wash their faces and their heads daily with the dirtiest and smelliest water. The slave girl (or maid) appears every morning with a big vessel full of water and offers it to her master. He washes his hands, face, and hair in it, combing it over the vessel. Then he blows his nose and spits in it. When he has finished, the girl takes the vessel to the next, who does the same as the other. She then passes from one to the next until all who live in that house have had their chance, each blowing his nose and spitting in it, as well as washing his face and hair [my translation].

See *Risa:lat Ibn FaDla:n*, ed. Sami al-Dahhan (Damascus: Al-Majma? al-?Ilmi: al-?Arabi: bi-Dimashq, A.D. 1959 [A.H. 1379]), p. 152.

the enemy in the hope that "their hearts would melt," as he used to say.

All of a sudden I break out laughing over the song that says, "Water will quench the thirst of the thirsty." "How did the singer arrive at this stunning discovery?" I ask myself. In Tel Zaatar, the killers used to hunt Palestinian women at the spring, at the broken water pipe, as if hunting thirsty gazelles.[11] Killer water. Water mixed with the blood of the thirsty who risked their lives for a cup of it. Water that lit the fires of war among the Bedouins in times gone by. Water good for improving the negotiating position of those whose dried-up humanity hasn't been melted by water. Water that got Arab kings moving, saddling them with the burden of getting in touch with the American president by phone to make a profitable deal: Take the oil, give us water. Take us, but give us water!

The sound of water is a wedding celebration louder, much louder, than the roar of these jets. The sound of water is a mirror for the living roots of the earth. The sound of water is freedom. The sound of water is humanity itself.

And no sooner did the White House in Washington announce that the water had been turned on again in West Beirut than people rushed to their taps. All except us, the tenants of

---

11.   Tel Zaatar was a Palestinian refugee camp in East Beirut, the region traditionally controlled by the Maronites, to whom it fell on 12 August 1976, in the heat of the Lebanese civil war. Cf. Gilmour, *Lebanon: The Fractured Country*, p. 140:

> There was little water in the camp and what there was in the wells was polluted. By the beginning of August hundreds of people had died and most of the survivors had dysentery. . . . But most of the camp's inhabitants remained and waited for the end. It came on 12 August when the Tigers and the Phalangists [Maronite militias] stormed in after a siege of fifty-three days. Over a thousand people were killed in the final assault; even more were lined up and shot immediately afterwards.

this tall building rising to the highest call of thirst. Its owner had put us under siege several years before Beirut itself came under siege. When authority in the country collapsed, he went mad with his own authority—power over water. Whenever he had a quarrel with one of his tenants, his wife, or his bank account, he rushed to cut off the water for all of us. For that reason, he had long ago instilled in us a patience for water. He had led us to value water and had taught us to feel a greater joy when it gushed for an hour than all the desert tribes of Dahis had ever felt. He had transformed us into watchmen over water pipes, alert from dawn for the sound of the awaited water. And when we heard the water gurgle, we declared a holiday and stored what we could in pots and pans, bottles and dishes, cups and glasses, and in the pockets of leather jackets. For water in this building was a treasure to be celebrated with rituals and discussed at evening get-togethers. Talk of water had united us and turned us into one family. But the owner of the building was jealous of Ariel Sharon, and competed with him in sadism. When West Beirut rejoiced over the release of the water, we had to be content with mere solidarity, because the water did not reach us and their joy did not include us. "We're the last prisoners, O landord. Forgive us sins we haven't committed, O Abu Rabi'. There's a war going on, O landlord. Be magnanimous, O Abu Rabi'. Give us our share of the water, O landlord." But no one heard, and no one came to intercede for us, until I turned to the armed people's committees for help. They came and released the water by force, and from sheer joy over the water we forgot about the war and the siege.

| | | | | | |

For me, and others like me who have burned with the wounds of water, Ibn Sida has set out the names of water and its attributes. What follows is only a drop from that flood:

water, waters, waterfall, rapids, cataract, cascade, snow, ice, hail, backwater, backwash, aqueduct, canal, droplet, drop, drizzle, cloudburst, rain, shower, torrent, soaker, spate, flood, deluge, mist, dew, steam, condensation, humidity, moisture, vapor, evaporation, aquifer, aquiclude, reservoir, freshet, brook, runnel, rill, rivulet, stream, creek, river, tributary, confluence, inlet, reach, slough, swamp, marsh, fen, puddle, pond, pool, tarn, lake, lagoon, cove, current, wave, eddy, whirlpool, undercurrent, billow, ripple, chop, surge, swell, spray, spurt, spout, squirt, splash, gurgle, gush, run, flow, meander, drip, ooze, seep, percolate, trickle, drop, leak, soak, drench, douse, dunk, dribble, inundate, saturate, irrigate, sprinkle, slosh, wash, dunk, dive, plunge, submerge, splatter, immerse, freeze, thaw, damp, wet, sodden, sopping, hydrous, aquatic, aqueous, watery.[12]

And many others.

| | | | | | |

I come down the long stone stairway, in the midst of smashed glass. I don't know if the lower floors have been hit. "What will I do if a corpse should fall on me?" I ask myself. "How will I carry it, and to whom shall I take it? What will I do if I find no one to talk to? To whom shall I bring my words, and who will

---

12. From *Al-MukhaSSaS*, by Ibn Sida. Rather than translate Ibn Sida literally, I have aimed for an equivalent effect.

share my silence?" I'll whistle a tune, the opening of a song dedicated to Beirut, exploding in this war. Beirut has not been the subject of song, and Lebanese poetry has not used the word "Beirut," though it fits into all the Arabic meters. A musical name which can flow smoothly into a verse or a prose poem.

What will I do if I don't find a kitten to play with? And what will I do if I find nothing to do?

On the fourth floor, an open door. "Good morning, Sir!" Thus have I greeted him for the past ten years. Eighty years old. Handsome, calm, like a heart walking on two legs. He moved out of his house on the demarcation line after three of its walls had fallen down and lived in my apartment for six months while I was hiding in Europe. Then he moved to his daughter's apartment.

I visit him daily, helping to lift from him the burden of the war, bringing him a newspaper and a sesame-covered bun. He had been an innovative poet; perhaps he was the first to use the form of the prose poem. Then he stopped writing poetry altogether, to devote himself full-time to his literary monthly. He is now editor, manuscript reader, administrator, and distributor. Nothing equals his grumbling about the savagery of the shelling except his complaints about the landlord and the water. He enjoys my company and that of his grandchildren, accepting the tyranny of his domineering wife with a smile that apologizes for a misdeed he didn't commit. When his nerves are on edge, he cries out with a pain brought on by the insistence of the raiding jets: "Enough! What do you want from us? We know you're stronger, and we know you have newer planes and more destructive weapons. So, what do you want from us? Enough!"

But his wife scolds him: "Let them be! They want to shell. What's it to you?" she says sharply in her Egyptian dialect, not feeling embarrassed by my presence: "They want to shell Palestinians." To interrupt the electric current of anguish, I joke with him: "That's right. Why do you want to put obstacles in the path of those pilots?" He laughs, but she doesn't. Within her, since she'd been brought up to feel hostile to anything outside her Maronite sect, she applauds the free service offered by the Israelis to the only hero of her dreams—Bashir Gemayel,[13] She believes this war's nothing more than a voluntary service they are rendering to clean Lebanon of aliens and Muslims. And when the service is complete, with Gemayel, the leader of the sect, elevated to the presidency of the republic after the aliens have been driven out, the Israelis will go back where they came from without asking a fee.

One can argue with her about the life of Jesus Christ, the Virgin Mary, and the Epistles of Paul, without her ever getting

13. Cf. Smith:

> By the end of 1980, Bashir Gemayel, younger son of Pierre, the patriarch of the Gemayel clan, had established his dominance over all the Maronite military forces. Gemayel had long been in contact with Israeli leaders, hoping to use them to realize his ambitions. Many of his assistants had received extensive training in Israel during and following Israeli intervention on the side of the Maronites in 1976. In Lebanon, Bashir Gemayel was backed by the Maronite religious establishment, now centered in the monastic orders which themselves contributed fighters to paramilitary groups. (*Palestine and the Arab-Israeli Conflict*, p. 261)

And Gilmour:

> Two days after the withdrawal of the Palestinians began, Bachir [sic] Gemayel was chosen as president by sixty-two deputies. This event was just as much a consequence of the Israeli invasion as the evacuation of the PLO, because in normal times Gemayel would not have received more than the twenty or so votes belonging to the Phalangists and Chamoun's National Liberal Party. (*Lebanon: The Fractured Country*, p. 171)

excited. But as for Bashir, she surrounds his name with an aura of sacrosanct taboo. *O Lady of Lebanon, protect him for us!* For all that, I feel no rancor toward her; rather, pity at how deeply she has gone into mere fantasy and refusal of the Other. I don't hold a grudge against her but bring her what bread and grapes I can find at the vendors. Before a mind so closed, so completely made up, all attempts at argument come to a halt. In vain does her husband, whose past is secular, try to convince her that the Israelis don't love Lebanon and aren't there to defend it, and that just one rocket from their jets can turn all of us sitting in this apartment, Muslim and Maronite alike, into ground meat. As for her, armed with a mind made up with such finality, she loves a sterile argument.

In an attempt to take my side, her husband occasionally asks my opinion, but to avoid provocation and whatever bile she might want to shower me with, I say, "It's not my problem."

She stirs the stagnant water, "What then is your problem?"

I maneuver. "My problem is to know what my problem is. By the way, has the landlord released the water?"

Says she, "Don't run away from the subject. You know there's no problem between Maronites and Jews."

I say, "I don't know that."

Says she, "You know we're allies."

I say, "I don't know that."

Says she, "What do you know then?"

I say, "I know water has color, flavor, and aroma."

Says she, "Why don't you Palestinians go back to your country? Then the problem will be over."

I say, "Just like that? So easy? We go back to our country, and the problem is gone?"

Says she, "Yes."

I say, "Don't you know they won't let us go back to our country?"

Says she, "In that case, fight them."

I say, "Here we are, fighting them. Aren't we at war?"

Says she, "You're fighting to stay here. You're not fighting to go back."

I say, "For us to go back there, we must be somewhere; because he who goes back—if he does go back—doesn't start from nowhere."

Says she, "Why don't you stay in the Arab countries and fight from there?"

I say, "They said to us what you're saying now. They kicked us out. And here we are, fighting along with the Lebanese in defense of Beirut and our very existence."

Says she, "Your war's pointless and will get you nowhere."

I say, "Perhaps it won't get us anywhere, but its aim is self-defense."

Says she, "You must leave."

I say, "We've already agreed to leave. We will leave. And here they are, barring us from leaving. But don't you care where we're going?"

Says she, "It doesn't concern me."

Suddenly, Feiruz's voice rises from the radio, *I love you, O Lebanon*. It rises from two warring stations.

I say, "Don't you love this song?"

She says, "I love it, and you?"

I say, "I love it very much, and it hurts me."

She says, "By what right do you love it? Don't you see how far beyond the limit you Palestinians have gone?"

I say, "It's beautiful, and Lebanon is beautiful. That's all there is to it."

She says, "You've got to love Jerusalem."

I say, "I love Jerusalem. The Israelis love Jerusalem and sing for it. You love Jerusalem. Feiruz sings for Jerusalem. And Richard the Lion-Hearted loved Jerusalem. And . . ."

Says she, "I don't love Jerusalem."

| | | | | | |

The street. Seven o'clock. The horizon a huge egg made of steel. To whom shall I offer my innocent silence? The street has become wider. I walk slowly. Slowly, I walk. I walk slowly, that a jet fighter may not miss me. The void opens its jaws, but it doesn't swallow me. I move aimlessly, as if getting to know these streets for the first time and walking on them for the last time. A one-sided farewell. I'm the one walking in the funeral, and the one whose funeral it is.

Even one kitten. If I were to find a kitten. No sorrow. No joy. No beginning. No end. No anger. No contentment. No memory. No dream. No past. No tomorrow. No sound. No silence. No war. No peace. No life. No death. No *yes*. No *no*. The waves have married the rock mosses on a distant shore, and I've just emerged from this marriage, which has lasted a million years. I emerged, but I didn't know where I was. I didn't know my name, or the name of this place. I didn't know that I had the power to unsheathe one of my ribs and uncover a script for the dialogue of this absolute silence. What is my name? Who gave me my name? Who is going to call me Adam?

| | | | | |

. . . Then God, having created the Pen and commanded it, so that it wrote into being everything that will exist till the Day of Judgment, created delicate clouds—the mist which the Prophet (God bless and grant him salvation!) mentioned when asked by Abu Ruzayn al-'Uqaili, "Where was the Lord before he created creation?" And he answered, "In a fine mist, with air above him and air below. Then he created the Throne on the water."

I said, "This bears looking into, for it has already been said that God (exalted above all!) first created the Pen and said, 'Write!' and the Pen set to it within the hour. It has also been said that God, after he had created the Pen and it had written the world into being, created a fine mist. Now it is a fact that there can be no writing without an instrument to write with, and that is the Pen, and without something to write on, and that is the Tablet Preserved. It would therefore appear the the Tablet Preserved should have been mentioned after the Pen, but only God knows. It could be that no mention was made of it because its presence would have been understood as a necessary part of the expression."

The learned have disagreed concerning what God created after the mist. Al-Dahhak has it from Ibn Mazahim, who has it from Ibn Abbas, that God first created the Throne and sat on it. But others have said God first created water before he created the Throne, then he created the Throne, placing it upon the water.

And it has been related that God (exalted above all!),

after the Pen, created the Chair, then the Throne, then air, then darkness, then water, upon which he placed the Throne.

In my view, the statement—derived from one of Abu Ruzayn's traditions about the Prophet (God bless and grant him salvation!)—that the creation of water came before the creation of the Throne is closer to the truth. Further, it has been related (by Sa'ad Ibn Jubayr, who has it from Ibn Abbas) that water was riding on the wind when the Throne was created. If that is the case, then they were created before the Throne.

Another has said that God created the Pen a thousand years before he created anything else.

They have also differed about the day in which God (exalted above all!) began the creation of heaven and earth. Abdallah Ibn Salam, Ka'ab, al-Dahhak, and Mujahid say creation was begun on Sunday. Muhammad Ibn Ishaq said (and Abu Hurayra agrees) that creation was begun on Saturday.

And they have also differed about what was created each day. Thus Abdallah Ibn Salam related that God (exalted above all!) began creation on Sunday and created the planets on Sunday and Monday. Then he created foods and the high mountains on Tuesday and Wednesday and the heavens on Thursday and Friday. He finished his creation in the last hour of Friday, whereupon he created Adam (peace to him!), and that will also be the hour of the final judgment.

According to Akramah, Ibn Abbas maintained that God (exalted above all!) placed the firmament on four corners on the water two thousand years before creating the world; then the earth was rolled into place under the firmament.

According to al-Sariy, who had it from Abu Salih and
Abu Malik, (who had it from Ibn Abbas), and from Mur-
rah al-Hamadhani and Ibn Mas'oud, God (exalted above
all!) had his Throne on the water and did not create any-
thing before water. And when He wanted to bring creation
into being, He brought vapor out of the water, and when
it rose out of the water, the vapor towered above it and He
called it the sky. He dried up the water and made it into
earth, which He then split into seven planets in two days,
Sunday and Monday. He created the earth on a whale, and
the whale is the letter Nune which He (exalted above all!)
mentions in the Qur'an when he says, "Nune and the
Pen." The whale was in the water, and the water was over
a wide, smooth stone, and the stone was on the back of an
angel and the angel on a rock, and the rock was in the
wind. This was the rock mentioned by Luqman, which is
neither in the sky nor on earth. The whale moved, and the
earth was disturbed and shook, whereupon God set the
mountains on it and it stayed in place.

Ibn Abbas, al-Dahhak, Mujahid, Ka'ab, and others have
said that each of the six days in which God created heaven
and earth was like a thousand years.

The learned have also differed about day and night—
which was created before its partner. Some have said night
was created before day. And others have said day before
night, reasoning that when God (exalted above all!) was by
Himself—there being no night or day—His light lit up ev-
erything He created until He created night. Ibn Mas'oud
has said, "The Lord does not have day or night. The light
of the heavens is the luminance of his face." Ubaid Ibn
Umair al-Harithi has related, "Once I was visiting Ali

when Ibn al-Kawwa' asked him about the dark spot on the moon, and he said, 'It's a sign that has been erased.' "

In a long discourse which he had from Ibn Abbas, who had it from the Prophet (God bless and grant him salvation!), Abu Ja'far spoke of the creation of the sun and the moon and their movement. They are on two wheels, each with three hundred and sixty handles pulled by an equal number of angels. The sun and moon occasionally fall off the wheel into a sea between the sky and the earth, and that is their eclipse. The angels then pull them out, and that is their appearance after the eclipse.[14]

| | | | | | | |

I walk down the street, exactly in the middle, not caring to know where I'm going. As if I were sleepwalking. I don't come out of anything, and I don't go into anything. But the rage in my conflicting emotions rises higher than the roar of jets, which I ignore.

We did not understand Lebanon. We never understood Lebanon. We will not understand Lebanon. We will never understand Lebanon.

We saw in Lebanon only our own image in the polished stone—an imagination that re-creates the world in its shape, not because it is deluded, but because it needs a foothold for the vision. Something like making a video: we write the script and the dialogue; we design the scenario; we pick the actors, the cameraman, the director, and the producer; and we distribute

14. Ibn Athir, *Al-Ka:mil fi: al-Ta:ri:kh* (A Complete History); my translation.

the roles without realizing we are the ones being cast in them. When we see our faces and our blood on the screen, we applaud the image, forgetting it's of our own making. And by the time production goes into postproduction, we are only too ready to believe it is the Other who is pointing at us.

Was it within our power to see differently, to see anything other than what made it easy for us to set reality against its own materiality? Our morale is our infrastructure. In other words, we are standing Marx on his head and bringing Hegel back to stand on his feet with the devices of a Machiavelli who embraced Islam at the entrance to one of Saladin's tents.

Is it simply because Lebanon is like that—difficult to study and understand? Or is it because we had no tools for knowing Lebanon other than this manner of adapting?

I'm not so much getting entangled in answering as I'm forcing myself into a quandary. No one understands Lebanon. Not its supposed owners or its makers; not its destroyers or its builders; not its allies or its friends; and not those coming into it, or those leaving it. Is it because disjointed reality cannot be grasped, or because disjointed consciousness is unable to grasp?

And I don't want a correct answer as much as I want a correct question.

We understood nothing of Lebanon except a language that made known within us an instinct for survival and a kinship relation raised to the level of nationalist discourse by that great Egyptian, Gamal Abdel Nasser. In addressing the inhabitants of this Arab continent, now becoming a mosaic, he spoke to their acute sense of loss, naming the banks of the river in such a way as to disguise the mud there—sects and dregs of the Crusaders coming back to life in the darkness, under the ringing speeches.

But when the nationalist thesis collapsed, these sects put forth their own almost-shared language.[15]

Video.

To see only what was comfortable at a moment when the contingency of our existence was being transformed into a vision drawn from the grand discourse of Arab nationalism, and then to have the vision turned into a mere promise that gradually retreated from awareness until those representing the mainstream became a minority under siege.

Video.

Because now is not the time for prophets—not a time in which isolation can be transformed into a compass for truth or a minority (the residue of the majority's project) become a guiding light.

Video.

Because the June 1967 war, cooked up to be the end of Arabism, was transformed by Arab regimes (which helped concoct it) into an excuse for neutralizing an anger they could not hold back, rather than into the initial stages of an alternative based on the people's revenge. Thus they confirmed their deviation into regionalism and sectarianism.

Video.

Because the Marquis of Sidon, who was waiting for a dispensation from the pope to put his sister under a Muslim, or if

15. The nationalist thesis the author refers to here is that of Arab unity articulated by President Gamal Abdel Nasser of Egypt. With his death in 1970, the nationalist thesis collapsed. Many Arab intellectuals consider the June War of 1967 to have been a direct attack not only on Nasser's Egypt but on the nationalist thesis as well. The reason the author says the Arab regimes "helped concoct" this war is that some of them did not then, and do not now, subscribe to this thesis.

not his sister then his niece, was not suitable as a genuine ally against the English, who were holding Acre under siege.
Video.

Because the collapse of the center with the signing of a peace treaty guaranteeing the end of war has given the fringe an excuse to launch an attack against the heart of the question, transforming it from a cause to an issue of dissension and discord.[16]
Video.

Because the aim of partitioning the land into coast and mountain between Arab and Frank was not, under prevailing conditions, to guarantee for the Arabs whatever forts and terrain had remained in their hands but to grant the enemy a respite that enabled him to establish a pattern that sanctioned his transition from exception to rule.[17]
Video.

Because this rib of Arabia, the broken rib, has been summoned to court, accused of aggression against the comfort of the thrones by circulating words denied currency in Arab parts: *woman, opposition, book, political parties, parliament, liberty, pork, democracy, communism, secularism.*

16. The peace treaty referred to here is the Camp David Accord between Egypt, under Anwar Sadat, and Israel, under Menachem Begin, which opened the way for the Phalangist-Israeli alliance to attack the "heart of the question"— i.e., the Palestinians.

17. The word "Frank" basically means "European." It is used by the Arab people in a slightly contemptuous way to refer to Europeans who have come to the Arab world as conquerors. This usage probably originated during the Crusades, which figure heavily in this section, where the author is talking about the Arab accommodation to the occupation of the land (parts of Lebanon and Palestine) by the Crusaders, and in the rest of the book as well, where it is used as a metaphor for foreign occupation of Arab lands.

Video.

Because Palestine has been transformed from a homeland into a slogan, not for action but for use as a tool to make statements about events and to embellish the discourse of the coup d'état industry, heavy and light, until the marriage of the last female descendant of the Caliph.

On borders, war is declared on borders.

Therefore, we should not have seen in Lebanon anything other than what hope was able to fashion: the look of a heroism that, with the attack of the desert's sea on the small island of the spirit, radiated from those defending their magnificent despair against the closed shell's promise. The names of places get narrower and narrower, and shrink. From the great Arab homeland, stretching from the ocean to the Gulf, to something more restricted: Sharm al-Sheikh, Mount Hermon, the West Bank of the River Jordan, the girl's school in Nablus, the Shuja'iya Quarter in Gaza, Gallerie Sam'an, As'ad al-As'ad Street in Beirut, Taba Hotel in Sinai, Bir al-Abed here, Shatila Refugee Camp, the airport traffic circle, to the final barricade beyond which is the desert or the sea.

| | | | | | |

Hallowed be your hands, you who clutch the last stone and the last ember.

Hallowed be your hands, which, all by themselves, raise mountains from the ruins of the orphaned sea.

And may your scorched shadows turn into the ashes of a phoenix from which a new life will rise, that you may create from these ashes and yourselves a manger for a child to be born.

And may your names sprout sweet basil on a plain that stretches under your footsteps—a plain where a grain of wheat can find its way back to its stolen soil.

You who are rising within us like moons kneaded into shape by a generous blood that calls out to fort guards who have fled to enemy lines, with no answer except a mocking echo.

You're all alone!

From the traces of your footsteps—steps that don't march except over or under—we'll gather up the scattered islands now in conflict as a poet gathers the sparks flying off hooves galloping over flint.

And from the canopy of metallic hawks' feathers now falling on us we will show the tribes the limits of their names.

All alone!

Guard then, as you are doing, the cutting edge of the song against what blunts the heart in this narrow wilderness, narrow like an open space that doesn't look out from a window.

All alone!

Behind you, the sea; in front of you, the sea; to your right, the sea; and to your left, the sea, with no solid earth except this hand clutching a rock that is the earth itself.

All alone!

Lift up, then, another hundred cities over this rifle's hammer, and let old towns emerge from their stables and from under the dominion of locusts growing in the tents of the wild ass of the desert.

Show us the way to us, that we may rid ourselves of the burden of corpses that aren't our corpses, and rotten fruit dangling from a language not our language; that we may follow in our own footsteps, not those of Caesar, who robbed us of identity and path.

For us, no death is left except the death of death itself.

All alone!

You're defending the lineages of this coast against the mixup of meanings, that history shall not be made docile and the place a mere estate to be inherited.

Hallowed be your hands, you, clutching the last stone and the last ember!

| | | | | | |

—*Good-bye, sir.*
—*Where to?*
—*Madness.*
—*Which madness?*
—*Any madness, for I have turned into words.*

| | | | | | |

I'm in a fit of patriotic fervor.

Meanwhile, the occupied sky, sea, and pine mountains keep on shelling original fears and the saga of Adam's exit from Paradise, repeated in endless sagas of exodus. I no longer have a country: I no longer have a body. The shelling continues to shatter the songs of praise and the dialogue of death, stirring in the blood like a light consuming inane questions.

What am I searching for? A fullness of gunpowder and an indigestion of the soul's anger. The rockets penetrate my pores and come out safe. How powerful they are! As long as I'm breathing hell and sweating out an inferno, I no longer feel the

Gehenna meted out by the air. Yet I want to break into song. Yes, I want to sing to this burning day. I do want to sing. I want to find a language that transforms language itself into steel for the spirit—a language to use against these sparkling silver insects, these jets. I want to sing. I want a language that I can lean on and that can lean on me, that asks me to bear witness and that I can ask to bear witness, to what power there is in us to overcome this cosmic isolation.

And I walk on.

I walk, to see myself walking, with firm steps, free even of myself, in the middle of the street, exactly in the middle. The flying monsters bark at me. They spit out their fire, but I'm indifferent. I hear only the rhythm of my footsteps on the cratered asphalt. And I see no one. What am I searching for? Nothing. Maybe what takes hold of my footsteps and strikes them against the sleeping streets is an unyielding resistance that hides the fear of loneliness, or the fear of death in the rubble. Never before have I seen Beirut in such profound morning slumber. For the first time, I'm seeing the sidewalks: clear sidewalks. For the first time I'm seeing the trees, visible trees with trunks, branches, and perennially green leaves. Is Beirut beautiful in itself?

Movement, arguments, crowds, and the hubbub of commerce used to hide this perception, transforming Beirut from a city to a concept, a meaning, an expression, a sign. This city printed books, distributed newspapers, and held seminars and conferences to solve the world's problems, but paid no attention to itself. It was busy sticking out a mocking tongue at the sand and the repression on all sides of it. It was a workshop for freedom. Its walls carried an encyclopedia of the modern world: it was a factory for making posters.

It was no doubt the first city in the world to upgrade the making of posters to the level of the daily paper. Perhaps its expressive powers, formed from a mixture of death, chaos, freedom, alienation, migration, and peoples, had become so full and had so overflown the known forms of utterance that it found only the poster capable of making room for powers of expression that went beyond the merely quotidian. Thus the poster became a recurrent term; in poems and stories it was used to convey the sense of something special. Faces on the walls—martyrs freshly emerging from life and the printing presses, a death which is a remake of itself. One martyr replacing the face of another, taking his place on the wall, until displaced by yet another, or by rain. Slogans that change place with other slogans, or wipe them out. Slogans that classify national priorities and the daily duties of states. Everything that passed in the world also passed through here, sometimes reflecting what went on outside, sometimes setting a pattern for it. If two intellectuals got into an argument in Paris, their dispute could turn into an armed encounter here. Because Beirut had to be in solidarity and up-to-date with everything new, with every old thing that renewed itself, and with each new movement or theory. A cinema of revolutions in speeded-up motion. Video for instant application. The new leader or new star in any field was nominated as Beirut's leader or star. Its walls were teeming with pictures and words, and passersby had to catch their breath from an experience that kept shifting.

Therefore, the reign of stars and leaders was short here, not because the audience was easily bored—the audience in fact was not here—but because the race was run on the American pattern even if its goals were anti-American. What we had were permanent representatives of every new consciousness, every new tune, and every new trend: the girl in jeans with a cigarette lighter dangling from a chain around her neck to project an immoderate leftism, the veil covering face and hands to indicate authenticity, or the seizing upon any sign that made an Orientalist of Karl Marx to prove that the winds of the East were now blowing. This was Beirut: the global transformer station that converted every deviation from the norm into a program of action for a public busy securing water and bread, and burying the dead.

| | | | | | |

I walk a street where no one is walking. I remember that before, I had walked a street no one had walked. And I remember that someone who was not with me had said:

—*Stop this dialogue, and come with me.*

—*Where to?*

—*To see this man.*

—*What's this man doing?*

—*Going home.*

—*But he's moving forward, then backward.*

—*That's his way of walking.*

—*He's not walking. He's swinging. He's dancing.*

—*Watch him closely. Count his steps: one, two, four, seven, nine forward. One two three, seven, eight backward.*

—*What does this mean?*

—*He's walking. This is the only way he knows to get home: ten steps forward and nine backward. That is, he advances by one step.*

—*What if his mind wandered, and he made a mistake in
the count?*
—*In that case he wouldn't get home.*
—*Do you mean anything by this?*
—*No. Nothing.*

| | | | | | | |

Near the Hotel Cavalier I look at my watch: eight o'clock. Is the
poet Y awake? Who can sleep, with these packs of fighter jets
above? I'm curious to know how a poet can write, how he can
find the words for this language. Y writes a daily poem that is
leisurely and visual, and he can capture details that suggest a
human essence. He's a poet who can coax joy out of the rubble,
and he can astonish. And when he writes, he makes it unneces-
sary for me to do so because he says on our behalf what we
ourselves would wish to say. He fills me with a sadness whose
purity awakens in me the very substance of happiness. And as
long as this poet is writing, I won't be able to find tangible evi-
dence for a crisis in poetry. In short, he's my kind of poet.

When I first met him in Baghdad, he tried to kill me: the
drinks he had at dinner didn't mix except to quarrel. He didn't
acknowledge any differences among drinks. All alcohols were
the same. No difference between beer, whiskey, wine, arak,
gin—all drinks made you lose your mind. And when, toward
the end of the evening, he drove us back to the Hotel Baghdad,
he would have taken both car and occupants for a swim in the
River Tigris but for our wide-awake cries of alarm. "Don't
worry," he said, calming our fears. "I'm now an employee of the
Department of Irrigation." "Irrigation?" we asked. "Yes, irriga-
tion," he answered. "Irrigation."

Eventually, he moved from the Department of Irrigation in Baghdad to the Department of Blood in Beirut. We held poetry-reading evenings together in Beirut and Damascus and, a few weeks ago, at a fedayeen base in Tyre. Last night, I saw him near the Plaza Hotel. In the darkness of the night he made out my face with a flashlight and screamed, "Why are you going about alone, without a bodyguard?" "When have I ever gone about with a bodyguard?" I asked. "Then what are you doing here?" he asked. "I'm waiting for a taxi so I can go to the war room," I replied.

| | | | | | | |

I'm waiting in the hotel lobby for the poet. But why is this snail looming before me? A tall snail. A snail that doesn't hesitate to show off its flaccid form. It sports on the sofa and the walls, letting its green spittle dribble over a young lady playing the piano. A snail that cries. A snail that laughs. A snail that gets drunk. It goes into the screen. It comes out of the screen. It fastens its wandering glance on nothing. A snail that doesn't look. It collapses. Sways. Bends. Flexes. Sighs. Falls apart. Loiters. A snail that moves about on teetering rubber feet. And why should the snail be looming in my face this morning? God protect us from the ugliness of such a sight!

| | | | | | | |

The poet comes down from his room leaning on a locust. *What! This one too! Why did I ever come here?* We embrace. I pat his shoulder to shake away the heaven of sleep. "How are you?" "Pessimistic. This is a strange day, brother! Incredible! They haven't stopped shelling for a single moment. They're plowing up the sky. Where were you?" "In my apartment." "Crazy. Are you out of your mind, my friend? How could you sleep there?" "Tomorrow I'm going to sleep here. But isn't this all we need, that the fruit of this shelling should be a snail and a locust?" "What do you mean?" "I don't mean anything." *Ten steps forward, and nine back. The net gain is one step forward. Good! This is good!*

Another locust, a frightened one, lands in my lap. Putting on an air of chastity provoked by fear of the jets, she rubs against whatever can be rubbed against. I say to her, joking, advising: "This is going to be a day without end. They have a thousand jets, which can make ten thousand sorties, and if you keep responding to each sortie with this rubbing, I'm going to dry up. I'll become a spent man." I turn to the poet: "Tell me, why do young women get excited under the worst conditions? Is this a time for love? This is no time for love, but for sudden desire. Two fleeting bodies collaborate to hold back one fleeting death by means of another—a honeyed death."

Our great friend F comes over to help me lift the poet out of a phrase he's fallen into: "Brother, this is impossible. Impossible. Brother, this is absolutely impossible." He's come to blows with the expression, choked, and piled on top of it. *Help me, F, Help me free the expression from Y's stammering.* We burst out laughing. We laugh and laugh till we upset the young lady at the piano. "This isn't the time for the piano, for laughter, or for poetry," we say to her. "This is the time for jets. It's the time for snails."

"Are both of you writing?" F asks.

Y writes every day. He reads us one of the snapshots from his sensitive internal camera, which he never goes without.

"And you?" they ask me.

"I'm stocking up," I say, "to the point of choking. And I'm mocked by friends who say, 'What use is poetry? What use will it be when the war ends?' But I'm screaming at a moment when screams can go nowhere. And it strikes me that language must force itself into a battle in which the voices are not equal. Your subdued voice is better, Y."

—But, what are you writing?

"I'm stammering out a scream," I answer:

Our stumps: our names
No. There is no escape!
Fallen, the mask over the mask
That covers the mask.
Fallen is the mask!
You've no brothers, my brother,
No friends, no forts, my friend.
You've no water and no cure
No sky, no blood, and no sails.
No front, and no rear.

Block your blockade then. No escape!
Your arm falls?
Pick it up and strike your enemy! No escape!
I fall beside you? Pick me up
And strike your enemy.
You are free now
Free,
Free.
Your dead and wounded
Are your weapons
Strike with them. Strike your enemy.

Our stumps, our names; our names, our stumps.
Block your blockade with madness
With madness
And with madness
They have gone, the ones you love. Gone.
You will either have to be
Or you will not be.
Fallen, the mask covering the mask
That covers the mask
Has fallen, and there's no one

None but you in this stretch of space
Open to enemies and forgetfulness.
Let every gun emplacement then
Be your home.
No! No one!
The mask has fallen.
Arabs who obeyed their Franks
Arabs who sold their souls
Arabs who are lost
Fallen is the mask
The mask has fallen.[18]

"Where will you two go?" F asks.

"To Aden," Y says.

"And you?" he asks me.

"I don't know," I answer.

Silence. Heavy as metal. We were three, but have now become one in the world crashing down around us. It's as if we

18. This is part of a larger poem Darwish wrote, apparently during the siege of Beirut, and published in *Al Karmel*, no. 7 (1983), under the title "In Praise of the Tall Shadow" *(madi:H al-DHill al-ʔa:li:)*. It was anthologized in *HaSa:r li mada: 'iH al-baHr* (Sea Elegies under Siege) (Tunis: CERES, 1984).

were here as caretakers of fragile substances and were now pre-
paring to absorb the operation of moving our reality, in its
entirety, into the domain of memories forming within sight of
us. And as we move away, we can see ourselves turning into
memories. We are these memories. As of this moment, we'll
remember each other as we'll remember a distant world disap-
pearing into a blueness more blue than it used to be. We'll part
in the pitch of longing. All three of us know the truth: we will
pull out of Beirut. And we know a hardship that is so hard no
one dares be seen in the act of seeing it: the people are with us
precisely because we are leaving.

"I won't be leaving," I say, "because I don't know where to
go. And because I don't know where I'll be going, I won't leave."

"And you?" I ask F.

"I'm staying. I'm Lebanese, and this is my country. Where
am I to go?"

I am embarrassed by my question, and by the extent to
which Beirut has become my song and the song of everyone
without a homeland. And I am embarrassed by the great ambi-
guity of the Idea.

| | | | | | |

That same day Jesus went out of the house and sat beside
the sea. And great crowds gathered about him, so that he
got into a boat and sat there; and the whole crowd sat on
the beach. And he told them many things in parables, say-
ing: "A sower went out to sow. And as he sowed, some
seeds fell along the path, and the birds came and devoured
them. Other seeds fell on rocky ground, where they had
not much soil, and immediately they sprang up, since they

had no depth of soil, but when the sun rose they were
scorched; and since they had no root they withered away.
Other seeds fell upon thorns, and the thorns grew up and
choked them. Other seeds fell on good soil and brought
forth grain. . . ."

And Jesus went away from there and withdrew to the
district of Tyre and Sidon. And behold, a Canaanite
woman from that region came out and cried, "Have mercy
on me, O Lord, Son of David; my daughter is severely pos-
sessed by a demon." But he did not answer her a word.
And his disciples came and begged him, saying, "Send her
away, for she is crying after us." He answered, "I was sent
only to the lost sheep of the house of Israel." But she came
and knelt before him, saying, "Lord, help me." And he an-
swered, "It is not fair to take the children's bread and
throw it to the dogs." She said, "Yes, Lord, yet even the
dogs eat the crumbs that fall from the master's table."
Then Jesus answered her, "O woman, great is your faith!
Be it done for you as you desire." And her daughter was
healed instantly.[19]

| | | | | | | |

At the Hotel Commodore, the stronghold of foreign journalists,
an American newsman questions me: "What are you writing in
this war, Poet?"

—I'm writing my silence.

—Do you mean that now the guns should speak?

—Yes. Their sound is louder than my voice.

—What are you doing then?

19. Matthew 13:1–8 and 14:21–28. Revised Standard Version.

—I'm calling for steadfastness.

—And will you win this war?

—No. The important thing is to hold on. Holding on is a victory in itself.

—And what after that?

—A new age will start.

—And when will you go back to writing poetry?

—When the guns quiet down a little. When I explode my silence, which is full of all these voices. When I find the appropriate language.

—Is there no role for you then?

—No. No role for me in poetry now. My role is outside the poem. My role is to be here, with citizens and fighters.

Some intellectuals found the siege an appropriate time for settling accounts and pointed their poisonous pens at their colleagues' chests. In vain did we shout, "Drop these petty matters! It's not the writers who have Beirut under siege, and it's not their laxity or flight that brings these buildings down over their dwellers. At worst, these writings of yours are not literature, and at best they're not anti-aircraft guns." "No," they said. "This is the first and final test of whether a writer or a poem is revolutionary. Either the poem is to be born now, or it will lose its right to be born."

"Then why did you allow Homer to write the *Iliad* and the *Odyssey?*" we teased them. "And why did you give permission to Aeschylus, Euripides, Aristophanes, Tolstoy, and others? Not everyone reacts the same way, writers! He who can write now, let him write now! And he who can write later, let him write later! And if you'll permit me to say what I think—without accusing anybody—I say the wounded, the thirsty, and those in search of water, bread, or shelter are not asking for poetry. And the fighters pay no heed to your lyrics. Sing if you wish, or hold your tongue if you want: we're marginal in war. But it is within our power to offer the people other services: a twenty-liter can of water is worth the Valley of Genius itself.[20] What is needed now is human commitment, not beauty in creative expression. Therefore, enough of your character assassinations! So what if the nerves of the critic collapsed and he left Beirut? And if the dramatist was too scared to cross the street? And the poet had lost some of his rhythm? Is it because the critic was not an admirer of your poetry and plays that you've put him under siege and are now shelling him with slander?"

In response to cultural residues within us that link the war cry to stirring verse—survivals that assume the poet's role is that of a commentator on events, an inciter to *jihad*, or a war correspondent—the Arabic literary milieu has become used to posing the question of poetry in the middle of raging war. In every battle they raise the question, "Where's the poem?" The political conception of poetry has become confused with the notion of event, regardless of historical context.

And at this particular moment, with jets plowing our bodies, these intellectuals, hovering over a missing body, are demanding poems that match air raids or at least upset the balance of forces. If the poem is not born "now," then when will it be born? And if it's to be born later, what value has it "now"? A question both easy and difficult, in need of a complex answer, like being permitted to say, for example, that a poem may be

20. The "Valley [or stream] of Genius" (Wadi Abqar) is a legendary place inhabited by the jinn.

born in a certain place, in a certain language and body, but that
it does not reach throat and paper. An innocent question, need-
ing an innocent answer, except that—in this company—it is
filled with the desire to assassinate the poet who dares to an-
nounce he is writing his silence.

It is galling that we should be ready during these air raids
to steal time for all this chatter, defending the role of the poet
whose writing is unique because it is rooted in his relation-
ship to the actual as it unfolds, that we should be doing this
at a moment in which everything has stopped talking, a mo-
ment of shared creativity when the people's epic is shaping
its own history. Beirut itself is the writing, rousing and cre-
ative. Its true poets and singers are its people and fighters, who
don't need to be entertained or spurred by a lute with broken
strings. They are the genuine founders of a writing that for a
long, long time will have to search for a linguistic equivalent to
their heroism and their amazing lives. How then can the new
writing—which needs time enough for leisure—crystallize and
take form in a battle that has such a rhythm of rockets? And
how can traditional verse—and all verse is traditional at this
moment—define the poetry now fermenting in the belly of the
volcano?

Patience, intellectuals! For the question of life and death
which is now supreme, the question of a will committing all its
weapons to the battlefield, the question of an existence taking
its divine and material shape—these are more important than
ethical questions about the role of poetry and the poet. And it is
fitting that we should honor the awe which these hours unfold,
the hours of the transfer of human existence from one shore to

another and from one state of being to another. It is fitting also that traditional poetry should know how to hold its humble silence in the presence of this newborn. And if it becomes necessary for intellectuals to turn into snipers, then let them snipe at their old concepts, their old questions, and their old ethics. We are not now to describe, as much as we are to be described. We're being born totally, or else dying totally.

Yet our great friend from Pakistan, Fayiz Ahmad Fayiz, is busy with another question: "Where are the artists?"

"Which artists, Fayiz?" I ask.

"The artists of Beirut."

"What do you want from them?"

"To draw this war on the walls of the city."

"What's come over you?" I exclaim. "Don't you see the walls tumbling?"

| | | | | | |

Why do I see a peacock, this aging peacock, tottering with his ivory stick, armed with two revolvers, puffed up with pride, drunk with scorn, and fascinated by a crown of spittle?

Why do I see this aging peacock, thief of colored feathers, bribing me with an inhibited smile while planting a dagger in my spine?

Why do I see this aging peacock flinging the scent of sweat and arak at me, trying to kiss my shoe to slip a grave under it?

Why do I see this aging peacock reaching for a chair and the wall, to gain a view over my heart, steal the sadness of lemons, and smuggle it to the captain of a ship that never arrives, mistaking it for Noah's ark, which has not yet arrived?

Why do I see this aging peacock adorned with the shoe of a slaughtered horse, taking it for a medal of honor?

Why do I see this aging peacock armed with two revolvers: one for killing me and the other for his own greedy butt?

Why do I see this aging peacock?

Why do I see the peacock?

Why do I see?

Why?

| | | | | | |

My study has burned. A shell from the sea turned it into a charcoal warehouse. It burned a few hours before we arrived. Where are we to find another place to carry on with our prattle? Our eternal calling in war or truce—chatter. Where can we carry on with it? Are we going to withdraw, or not? The intellectuals consider the question theirs, and it's marvelous to behold their energies fuse into a plan for holding on. They believe they have the right to veto this political decision. Some of them are convinced that the publication of *Al-Ma'raka* (The Battle) will decide the fate of this battle.[21] They've decided this valiant pulpit will be history's witness that they are the ones controlling its twists. How beautiful they are! How beautiful!

It's eleven o'clock, twenty thousand shells, and thirty seconds. We walk out of the burning office into a sky ablaze. The sky hugs the earth with a smoky embrace. It hangs down, heavy with molten lead, a dark gray whose nothingness can only be penetrated by the orange leaked from jets whose silver flashes to

21. *Al-Ma'raka* (The Battle), a publication "issued by the Palestinian, Lebanese, and Arab writers and journalists in Beirut," covered the events of the siege of Beirut, appearing daily from 23 June to 25 August 1982.

a blazing whiteness. Graceful airplanes, slender, riding securely
the furrowed air.

"Let's go!" says Z.

"Where?" I ask.

"To look for something," he says. "Lunch, for example."

What's the situation? Terrible. The conditions for with-
drawal are humiliating, and we're maneuvering, trying to buy
time. At what price? At any price. With anti-aircraft guns out of
ammunition. With the heroism of young men who have baffled
military science and madness. For how long? Until something
that can't happen happens. Nothing has changed. We're still
alone. Will they venture into Beirut? No, they won't. They'll take
such heavy losses that they won't be able to bear the conse-
quences. But they're trying to bite off the edges of the city. They
tried near the museum, and failed. The morale of the defenders
is high, very high. They're like devils. They've given up on help
from outside. They've given up on any movement from the Arab
world. They've given up on the strategic balance.[22] Therefore,
they fight as if possessed. Has talk of withdrawal reached them?
Yes, but they don't believe it. It's only a maneuver, they say, and
they fight on. And they realize that the silence now crowning
the world offers them a pulpit from which to speak. Their blood,
and only their blood, is what speaks these days. What shall we
write in Al-Ma'raka about this talk of negotiations and with-
drawal? We call for fighting and holding on; we call for holding
on and fighting.

22. The "strategic balance" is a buzzword for what may be called the
"Assad Doctrine" (after Hafez Assad, president of the Syrian Arab Republic),
according to which it is unwise to engage Israel militarily before achieving a
strategic balance—i.e., military parity—with it.

Beirut from the outside, surrounded by Israeli tanks and official Arab paralysis, has been plunged into darkness and blackmail. Beirut is thirsty.

Yet the Beirut of the inside, Beirut from the inside, prepares its other reality. It holds its nerve. It raises its guns to protect the radiance of its meaning as the capital of Arab hope.

It was intended by those raising the motto "Save Beirut!"— demonic and glib, and fatal like a soft poison—that this hope should kill itself in an *Arab* Masada, the story of those going to their suicide at the zenith of their victory. The only condition the inventors of the slogan "Save Beirut!" are laying down is surrender. The surrender of a history of meanings watered with blood. Surrender of the totality of anger. Surrender of all weapons. A surrender costing nothing.

But do the experts in the blackmail industry know the meaning of this despair, and what its consequences will be? We're not talking here of counter-blackmail, and we're not threatening to bring down the temple on ourselves, our enemies, and our allies. But we are putting on the negotiating table our only condition and our only freedom: that we go on fighting.

Beirut is not a hostage. And in Beirut, behind our barricades, we're not wagering our lives except on the future and the renewal of the blood circulating in the veins of all generations. Therefore, we have no choice except to insist on the present condition of our existence: our weapons. To give them up would disarm us of the implements of our existence, of our guardianship of a flame we lit in a forest of our blood, and our ability to wake up this Arab continent fast asleep under repressive regimes.

Our holding on in fortress Beirut, indestructible, is the only tool for rousing the Arab giant stretching between the shores of two oceans. It's the only horizon that looks out from the muzzle of a gun, from the hole in a fighter's boot, and from a wound that lights up this dark age.

Thus. Thus we're lifting the siege from Beirut, and from the anger of the millions.

Thus Beirut seen from the inside looks nothing like Beirut seen from the outside.

"Thus we used to write. What should we be writing now?"

"Exactly the same thing," said Z, without hesitation.

"And what does the general population think, the people of Beirut?"

"They're for holding on," he said.

"They're for holding on until we withdraw," I said. "Can we ignore that?"

"No," he said. "We can't ignore it. But what can we do? What can we do?"

| | ·| | | | | |

A sound out of the ordinary, not because it's more powerful than other sounds, but because it's different and distant. A sound that snatches the place and runs. A sound that cuts through space and hollows out light.

Let's go! We haven't been on the road to Raouche for some days now. A wide boulevard, deserted and appearing wider because no feet are treading it, as if it had become the property of the sea itself. Smoking buildings. Fire dropping from above. An upside-down conflagration. Windows that grow old and fall slowly down. Cries for help from the upper floors reach us, clear and piercing. Human beings besieged by fire and the rubble of the building gradually collapsing from the shock of the initial jolt. The first-aid people are there, trying to save human flesh kneaded into a paste with steel, cement, and glass.

I can't turn my face from the wounded spot. Blood on the ground and the walls has a savage pull. I can neither leave nor allay a feeling of helplessness. Heavy crowding. The civil defense orderlies ask us to leave because we're hindering their work, and because the jets will come back to graze on this appetizing crowd. Hot water, welling up from rage held back, wets my face. My friend takes me by the arm: "Come! Let's get out of here!"

They have raided again. Again they have raided. What is this day? Is it the longest day in history? I look to the building opposite, for a last glance at my study.

| | | | | | |

A wave from the sea. I used to follow it with my eyes from this balcony as it broke against the Raouche rock, famous for lovers' suicides.

A wave that carries a few last letters and returns to the blue northwest and azure southwest. It returns to its shores, embroidering itself with puffs of white cotton as it breaks.

A wave from the sea. I recognize it and follow it with longing. I see it tiring before it reaches Haifa or Andalusia. It tires and rests on the shores of the island of Cyprus.

A wave from the sea. It won't be me. And I, I won't be a wave from the sea.

| | | | | | |

How I used to love my study, threatened with destruction from the beginning! "What kind of present do you want?" *Plants and* roses. *Flowers and plants*. I made it into something like a nest. I wanted it to be like a text in a magazine: brown characters on yellow paper, and overlooking the sea. I wanted it to be a flowerpot fastened to the back of an untamed horse. I wanted it to be like a poem. But no sooner did we hang a painting than a car bomb exploded, destroying all the arrangements. And no sooner did I rest my head on my left elbow, waiting for my coffee, than I found myself outside. The roar of an explosion lifted me as I was, holding pen and cigarette, and left me safely in front of the elevator. I found a rose on my shirt. A minute later, I tried to get back into the study, which now, without its doors, had turned into a space full of broken glass and flying paper, but the force of the second explosion kept me near the elevator. The young guard answered the explosion with shots from his pistol. "What are you doing?" I asked. "I'm firing my gun," he answered. "What are you shooting at? Where is it?" I asked. Perhaps no one had ever asked him these questions before, and that was why he found them ridiculous. But that's how it's always been. Our immediate response, spontaneous and perhaps even instinctive, to any event or violent feeling—a news item or just being hit by a ball—is to fire our guns in the air.

A new massacre near Raouche: another twenty dead from this new fever, the fever of the car bomb, perfected by the Mossad and its local agents. These cars paved the way for the invasion. They prepared the psychological ground for turning this siege into a natural event. Modern Trojan horses, neighing into the general awareness that there was no safety or security in West Beirut. Every car parked by a sidewalk held the promise of death. Let the barbarians come in, then!

| | | | | | |

A wave from the sea in my hand. It seeps and trickles away. It works its way around the rock in my chest, comes close, relaxes, and surrenders. It clings to the hair on my chest, so as not to go back to its source. Hot and humid. A wave like a cat munching an apple. She then kisses me with the frivolity of a wanton: "I have a right to love you, and you have a right to love me." *Love is not a right, kitten, and I'm exactly forty.* She withdraws into a corner. "And I'm a feminine half-moon running after a male." Hot and humid. Yet the little body is temperature regulated, warm in winter and cool in summer. A fresh body like the shore of a new sea, whose mosses small animals have not yet touched. It slips, and moves away; it burns, and comes closer. The aroma of milk holds me away from it. "Why don't we hang August on a chair? Why don't we swim in the whiteness of sleep?" She covers her eyes that sparkle at night. *Because you're young.* "I'm not young," she roars. "I'm a feminine half-moon running after a male, following the aroma of cardamom. Don't I have the right to swim?" *But this whiteness is not a sea.* She gets angry and bites on an apple and her fingernails. I gather the two lips with my fingers so that they become larger, turning into a kiss. "There! You do love me. Confess you love me. Tell me you love me. Why then don't you drink my salt?" *Because thirst shatters the elegance of my spirit.* She gets angry, goes and squats in the corner: "I don't want poetry. I don't love poetry. I want the body. I want a piece of the body. Coward!" *A coward for your sake, not mine.* "What have you to do with what belongs to me? I'm free to do what I want with what I own." She stops. Gets closer. Her meow becomes coarser: "Give me something to play with! Give me a doll! Any doll. A small cat, taut and firm, over which I can pass my hands gently until its saliva flows over my breast."

The wave was about to drown, but a violent explosion shook the rocks in the sea. The wave flew to the road, and I flew to the bed.

| | | | | | |

For an hour now, I haven't exchanged a word with my friend Z. He's driving around aimlessly in his car. "Where are you?" we each ask the other. "I know where you've been," I say. "Tell the truth. Weren't you doing something naughty with the pilot's wife?" He's stunned: "How did you know?" "Because I too just came back from doing much the same," I say. "That's how I know where death takes us."

"It's time we ate," he says.

"Sardines again?" I ask.

"Anything," he answers.

This *anything* turns out to be not just anything. Suddenly, he stops his car and shouts: a lamb on a meat hook! We're at the beginning of Commodore Street, which leads to Raouche. We know the butcher. He doesn't act like a butcher—more like an undertaker. He attaches himself to any leader at any funeral, so as to appear in the photograph. "How full of paradoxes the Palestinian phenomenon is!" I say. "It's my good fortune I'm not a playwright, or I'd have to show the other side of the picture. Do you realize that the eye of the writer is negative, just like the ear of the leader? They're fascinated by a wounding paradox here, a slander there. Slander has spread in our political life in a ruinous way, a companion to the inflation of self, the bloating of the body, and the dwindling concern with asking questions. Whole offices have been opened, complete with air-conditioning, which are nothing more than parlors for slander and the spreading of rumors. Further, the martyr trade has flourished among some of the smaller factions: 'We need twenty more martyrs to fill the list, and an armed struggle over a martyr whose faction is not known. And the execution of a fighter who refused to shoot a friend who belonged to another faction. His body was thrown into an unused well, until discovered by a woman fortune teller. And . . .' "

Z interrupts me, "Tonight I'll show you the game of the camera and the shadow."

"I'm not interested," I say.

"Where shall we eat?" he asks. "We need some charcoal and a building where we can be fairly secure."

We are stunned to see the clear blue of the sky, not spoiled by jets. For a whole minute now there have been no jets. Have they grown tired?

The secure apartment in the somewhat-secure building fills with hungry friends. People spill out of their shelters. *No jets! No jets!* One of them asks, "Where are Bakhtin's books?" Another answers, "The critic who used to live in this apartment took them and ran away." Some try to defame him. Someone else says, "Enough! We're in need of a live Palestinian interested in Marxism and linguistics." They consider this a good opening for slander, except that a storm of jets walks over us, scattering us into the street and saving the reputation of the absent critic.

This rumble—we've never heard it before. Low, distant, deep, and secret, as if it had come from the belly of the earth, like the awesome sound of the Day of Judgment. All of us feel—

and we have by now become experts in the science of killer sounds—that something out of the ordinary, in this extraordinary war, is taking place. And that a new weapon is being tried out. When will this long day end? When will it end so we can find out if we're alive or dead?

The one carrying the meat says, "What shall we do with this leg?" We all ignore his greedy question. But he stupidly goes on asking it while we're busy looking for something that may help us gather our severed parts. He goes on until I say, "Take this meat to the nearest shelter, put a hole in it, make love to it, and let's have done with it and you!"

But that distant rumble stirs in us an ancient fear—the fear inspired by deep and primitive jungles. Z and I walk on, led by our fear. The scene near Sanaya Gardens is like a sight from Judgment Day. Hundreds of terrified people around an immense stone coffin. An apprehensive silence carrying the weight of metal under a sun veiled by all the colors of ash. We slip in among the crowd, looking for a place to peek over closely packed shoulders, a human fence held together by fear and anger. And we see—a building gulped by the earth: seized by the hands of the cosmic monster lying in ambush for a world that human beings create on an earth commanding no view except of a moon and a sun and an abyss, pushing humanity into a bottomless pit in peering over whose edge we realize we didn't learn to walk, read, or use our hands except to reach an end that we forget, only to carry on our search for something that can justify this comedy and cut the thread connecting the beginning with the end, letting us imagine we are an exception to the only truth.

What is the name of this thing?

A vacuum bomb.[23] It creates an immense emptiness that annihilates the base under the target, the resulting vacuum sucking the building down and turning it into a buried graveyard. No more, no less. And there, below, in the new realm, the form keeps its shape. The residents of the building keep their previous shapes and the varied forms of their final, choking, gestures. There, below, under what a moment ago was under them, they turn into statues made of flesh with not enough life for a farewell. Thus he who was asleep is still sleeping. He who was carrying a coffee tray is still carrying it. He who was opening a window is still opening it. He who was sucking at his mother's breast is still suckling. And he who was on top of his wife is still on top of her. But he who happened to be standing on the roof of the building can now shake the dust off his clothes and walk into the street without using the elevator, for the building is now

---

23. Cf. the following quotations from *Israel in Lebanon: Report of the International Commission to Enquire into Reported Violation of International Law by Israel during Its Invasion of the Lebanon* (London: Ithaca Press, 1983), pp. 86 and 47:

> The Commission received evidence and testimony as to the use by the IDF on at least one occasion of a weapon variously called the "fuel-air explosive," "concussion" or "vacuum bomb." The incident which appears to have alerted many people to the use of this weapon was the extraordinary total destruction of the buildings near the Sanaya Gardens by only two bombs without any of the usual accompanying destruction of objects nearby. Various descriptions of the working and effect of this bomb are to be found (e.g., Mr. Me'ir Cohen in *Ha'aretz*, 19 September 1982, Mr. Robik Rosenthal in *Al-Hamishmar*, 11 August 1982, John Bulloch, *The Daily Telegraph*, 9 August 1982).

And:

> A number of reputable reporters were near or at the scene of the destruction by bombing of an eight-storey complex of flats near the Sanaya Gardens in West Beirut on 6 August 1982. The Commission visited the site, now a large empty crater. . . . No ranking PLO official was in the building. On the contrary, we received evidence that the apartment block was of a civilian nature, and that the number of civilians who died in the ruins was estimated at 250.

level with the ground. For that reason the birds have remained alive, perched in their cages on the roof.

And why did they do this? The commander in chief had been there and had just left. But did he really leave? Our anxious question turned him from a father figure into a son. We didn't even have time to question the question. He'd been there. So what? Does that give them the right to exterminate a hundred people?

Another question is on our minds. Has he really managed to survive the repeated attempts to assassinate him with jets and advanced weapons like the vacuum bomb? Yesterday, he played chess in front of American cameras to push Begin into an excess of madness, to deprive him of grounds for political abuse and force him into racist vituperation: "These Palestinians are not human. They're animals who walk on all fours." He has to strip us of our humanity to justify killing us, for the killing of animals—unless they're dogs—is not forbidden in Western law. Begin was repeating the history of his madness and his crimes. He thought his soldiers, the hunters of these animals, were out on a hunting safari. But hundreds of coffins were thrown in his face, lifted by thousands shouting, "How much longer?" We're not human because we didn't allow him to occupy an Arab capital, and he can't believe mere human beings could stop the legend from becoming a court for judging all values and all humanity, at any time and place, an absolute and eternal court. He therefore had to transform those who resisted him into something inhuman, into animals, after the legend in which he believed had closed off all windows to an askable question, "Who really is the animal?" The ghosts of those he annihilated at Dayr Yasin, all those whom he made disappear from time

and place, so that through that absence he could impose the
conditions of his own presence on the time and the place—they
have now pounced on his dreams and his daydreams.[24] These
very ghosts, having heroically gained back flesh, bone, and spirit,
now have him under siege in Beirut. The ghost who was a victim
had come back a hero. Between ghost and hero, the prophet of
lies was besieged by a delusion that held him back from calling
on Old Testament books, which he thought could, on their own,
write the history of humanity.

| | | | | | |

The seventh time the priests blew the trumpets and Joshua
said to the army, "Shout! The Lord has given you the city.
The city shall be under solemn ban: everything in it be-
longs to the Lord. No one is to be spared except the prosti-
tute Rahab and everyone who is with her in the house,
because she hid the men we sent. And you must beware
of coveting anything that is forbidden under the ban; you
must take none of it for yourselves; this would put the Is-
raelite camp itself under the ban and bring trouble on it.
All the silver and gold, all the vessels of copper and iron,
shall be holy; they belong to the Lord and they must go
into the Lord's treasury." So they blew the trumpets, and
when the army heard the trumpet sound, they raised a

24.   Menachem Begin was the leader of the paramilitary organization Ir-
gun Zvai Leumi at the time of the Dayr Yasin massacre. See Smith, p. 143:

The village of Dayr Yasin overlooked the Jerusalem road, but it had ap-
parently entered into a non-aggression pact with the Haganah. Nevertheless,
a joint Irgun-LEHI force attacked the village, took it after quelling resistance,
and slaughtered about 250 men, women, and children whose mutilated bodies
were stuffed down wells. . . . The significance of Dayr Yasin went far beyond
its immediate fate.

great shout, and down fell the walls. The army advanced on the city, every man straight ahead, and took it. Under the ban they destroyed everything in the city; they put everyone to the sword, men and women, young and old, and also cattle, sheep and asses.

But the two men who had been sent out as spies were told by Joshua to go into the prostitute's house and bring out her and all who belonged to her, as they had sworn to do. So the young man went and brought out Rahab, her father and mother, her brothers and all who belonged to her. They brought out the whole family and left them outside the Israelite camp. They then set fire to the city and everything in it, except that they deposited the silver and gold and the vessels of copper and iron in the treasury of the Lord's house. Thus Joshua spared the lives of Rahab the prostitute, her household, and all who belonged to her because she had hidden the men whom Joshua had sent to Jericho as spies; she and her family settled permanently among the Israelites. It was then that Joshua laid this curse on Jericho: "May the Lord's curse light on the man who comes forward to rebuild the city of Jericho."[25]

| | | | | | |

The commander in chief was playing chess. He had mastered the game of playing with Begin's nerves, which dangled like electrical wires over the Ouza'i dump. On the chessboard, the man blockaded in Beirut put under siege that which he did not express publicly. The way we read it, he was laying siege to more than one piece on the board and more than one king who stood

25. Joshua 6:16–22. New English Bible.

outside the game. Speaking in images, he was making them
postpone their funeral orations, full as they were of tears—royal,
democratic, and people's democratic tears—that had been held
back for a month, ever since the Israeli advance had reassured
our official orators about the scope of an invasion (which they
had blessed with sublime indifference) proposed to guarantee
the safety of Galilee against the armed longing which the sons
of Galilee bear for the land of Galilee.

Was he here a moment ago? Has he left the place?

I happen to see one of his bodyguards who is not in the
habit of lying to me, and I become even more worried. "He
wasn't there," he whispers. "He had left." "And you too must
leave right away," he adds. "A crowd like this will only tempt
the aerial hunters to raid again."

This is the same young man who ran into me a few days
ago in one of the Organization's offices and whispered in my
ear, "Come with me!" I understood the signal, and didn't ask
where we were going. I expected anything except to find myself
face-to-face with this man of Germanic features sitting with the
Chief. "Do you remember me?" he asked. "I'm Uri." I was angry,
but I said in jest, "What! Have the Israelis conquered Beirut? Or
have you been taken prisoner?" "Neither one," he answered. "I
came over from Ashrafiya to interview Mr. Arafat for the press."
I became even more angry but made no comment. Beirut was
full of journalists from the world press. Was an interview with
this particular journalist necessary now? For every text there is a
context, and this was not the context for this text.

But Arafat had another perspective on how to manage in-
formation. Perhaps he wanted to send a message directly or to
make Begin wallow in a deeper madness. He was much calmer

than the message he wanted to send to the agitated Israeli public. When the journalist asked him where he'd be going after leaving Beirut, he answered without hesitation, "I'm going to my country. I'm going to Jerusalem." I was not as affected by this speech as the Israeli was. His eyes filled with tears of shame. "Why not?" Abu Ammar added. "Why shouldn't I go to my own country? Why should you have the right to go to my country and I not have the right to go back there?"

Silence.

The dialogue came to an end. The woman photographer and the journalist's female assistant looked more intently at the face of the legendary enemy. One of them asked, "Where is his famous kaffiyeh?" "It's everywhere," I answered. "But now he's wearing his military cap because he's in battle." She came even closer to him.

"You find him attractive?" I asked. "He's single."

"Yes," she answered, "very attractive."

As for me, I didn't like the interview, or the frivolity of the apartment owner, who thrust his family in front of the Israeli camera for no other reason than to let his family *there* have a look at the picture of his happiness *here*. I thought to myself, "It's our duty to know what we long for. Is it for the homeland? For our picture outside the homeland? Or for the picture of our longing for the homeland to be seen inside the homeland?"

| | | | | | |

Where is S, the neighborhood's eloquent rooster? Lover of pistols, language, and exposed flesh. I haven't seen him in two days. Has he been able to find food and water? That is my worry. Ever since I took him under my wing, he rarely speaks to me when

we're alone. Maybe he believes I'm his father. He moved out of
the neighborhood where he lived before the siege to share a
house here with a Lebanese youth of Chaldean origin.[26] Where
is the Chaldean fellow, and where is S, the Kurd? They became
friends the first day of the siege. One of them is as tense as a
muscle and the other cool, like the moon. S is always looking
for J, while J is searching for a way to disappear that would make
him appear a martyr. And when they meet, they curse each other
and then go walking the streets of Hamra armed to the teeth
with weapons and self-importance, as if guarding the air itself
against penetration or counter-revolution.

I've liked S ever since I found him several years ago in a
state of alert against some unknown. Too shy for talk, getting
nervous when he ventures into conversation. Firm, stern, and
never in a mood to bargain over what he thinks, or anything
else for that matter. He doesn't disclose the strange world within
him, except to the paper on his pillow. A fantasist, overflowing
with eloquence. I still don't know where the novelist in him
begins and the poet ends. He has taken the cultural life of Beirut
by storm, overnight. He defends his writing ferociously, with his
fists, because he doesn't believe in dialogue among intellectuals,
considering it mere babble. Taking his pistol and his showy
muscles, he goes into the appropriate coffee shop and lies in
wait for lesser critics who write for the cultural pages of daily
papers, and he doesn't mince his words about what they'd writ-
ten against him. One time I said to him, "Vladimir Mayakovsky

26. The Chaldeans are a Semitic people who belong to the Nestorian
branch of the Eastern Orthodox Church. There are communities of them scat-
tered throughout the Middle East, and they speak their own language, Syriac.
There is also a sizable community in the United States.

used to treat his critics the same way in Gorky Street." "This is the only true criticism of criticism," he answered.

S is elated by the war: it has allowed his repressed violence to emerge and ally itself with chaos. In war he gives his horses free rein, unsheathing the hooves of a song that scatters not dust but bullets. And in war he returns to the era of ancient mountains, to shepherds' pipes that make the distant dance, to chivalry and the din of self-conceit and the splendor of the first knights in armor. Briefly, in war he finds the battlefield of winds that unsheathe him, a fresh sword in a fencing match against enemies who have already passed through. And he does not understand. He does not understand why writers write in a war. Who pays them any heed at a moment when only power can speak? Slapping his pistol, he threatens: "We'll win! We'll rub their noses in the dirt!" He doesn't know whether he's going to win or not, for he's a child of the losing battle, the son born against reckoning. What matters to him is the challenge, the joust.

S stands somewhere between Don Quixote and Sancho, transforming enemies into abstractions ready at hand. He puffs up with patriotic fervor, rolls himself into a ball, stretches, tenses up, and lashes out at anything. But then he puts himself under the sway of J's wisdom—J the thoughtful, the enemy of lyricism in poetry, the seeker after its philosophical truth. S has found the "woman of matchless beauty" amid the general lack of water, meat, and women. *Take care, S, for she's the creation of your grandfather Don Quixote and the child of lizards that appear in the furrows of a soul cracked from thirst in the heat of midsummer days. Her voice is the voice of dried plants in the wilderness surrounding a ruin.* Yet S has taken a major and irreversible leap in the direction of a self-transformation cut off from its own truth, plunging deeply into comedy to attain what was missing in knight-errantry: a woman.

Where is S now? Did the shrapnel hunt him down, or did he himself hunt down a chicken to present to his "woman of matchless beauty?"

| | | | | | |

The vacuum bomb. Hiroshima. Manhunt by jet fighter. Vanquished remnants of the Nazi army in Berlin. A flaring up of the personal conflict between Begin and Nebuchadnezzar. Headlines that jumble past with present, urging the present to hurry on. A future sold in a lottery. A Greek fate lying in wait for young heroes. A public history with no owners, open to whoever wishes to inherit. On this day, on the anniversary of the Hiroshima bomb, they are trying out the vacuum bomb on our flesh, and the experiment is successful.

What I remember of Hiroshima is the American attempt to make it forget its name. I know Hiroshima. I was there nine years ago. In one of its squares, it spoke of its memory. Who will remind Hiroshima that Hiroshima was here? The Japanese interpreter asked if I'd seen the famous film, *Hiroshima mon amour*. I answered, "I can love a woman from Sodom, for love or play. I can love a body whose guards may kill me through the window." "I don't understand," she said. "It's just poetic fancy," I said. "But where is Hiroshima?" "Hiroshima's here," she answered. "You're in Hiroshima." "I don't see it," I said. "Why did you cover the name of its body with flowers? Is it because the American pilot cried later? He pushed a button, and saw nothing but a cloud. But when he saw photographs later, he cried."

"Such is life," she said. "But America didn't cry," I said. "She wasn't angry with herself. She was angered by the power balance."

Hiroshima tomorrow. Hiroshima is tomorrow.

There's nothing in the museum of the crime that points to the name of the killer: "The plane came this way, from a base in the Pacific." Is this collusion, or is it kowtowing? As for the victims, they need no names. Human skeletons bare of leaves. Branches made of bone, just for the shape. Forms, just for the form. A few locks of hair single out a woman over there. Inscriptions on the wall explain degrees of death—from burns, smoke, poison, or radiation. Preliminary exercises for a more comprehensive global killing. Preparing for the end. Nowadays, the Hiroshima bomb's destructive power makes it seem primitive nuclear weaponry. Yet it has enabled scientific imagination to write the scenario of the end of the world: an enormous explosion, a gigantic explosion that will resemble the initial formation of the globe with its organized chaos of mountains, wadis, plains, deserts, rivers, seas, slopes, lakes, wrinkles, rocks, all the beautiful variety of an earth glorified in poetic praises and religious ceremonies. After the giant explosion, a great fire will blaze, consuming whatever it can eat—human beings, trees, stones, and other things that can burn—and giving rise to a dense smoke that will blot out the sun for many days until the sky weeps a black rain, which they call nuclear rain, that will poison every living thing. The earth will then cool down and return to the Ice Age. And in the period of rapid transition from this age to the Ice Age nothing will remain alive except rats and certain types of insects. One morning the rats will wake up to find they are human beings who rule the earth. Kafka turned upside down. And I ask: Which is more cruel? That a human being should wake up to find he's a giant insect, or that an insect should wake up to find it is a human being who plays with an atomic bomb thinking it nothing more than a football?

| | | | | | |

The sky of Beirut is a huge dome made of dark sheet metal. All-encompassing noon spreads its leisure in the bones. The horizon is like a slate of clear gray, nothing coloring it save the playful jets. A Hiroshima sky. I can, if I want, take chalk in hand and write whatever I wish on the slate. A whim takes hold of me. What would I write if I were to go up to the roof of a tall building? "They shall not pass"? It's already been said. "May we face death, but long live the homeland"? That's been said before. "Hiroshima"? That too has been said. The letters have all slipped out of my memory and fingers. I've forgotten the alphabet. All I remember are these six letters: B-E-I-R-U-T.

| | | | | | |

I came to Beirut thirty-four years ago. I was six years old then. They put a cap on my head and left me in Al-Burj Square. It had a streetcar, and I rode the streetcar. It ran on two parallel lines made of iron. The streetcar went up I didn't know where. It ran on two iron lines. It moved forward. I couldn't tell what made this big, noisy toy move: the lines of iron laid on the ground or the wheels that rolled. I looked out the window of the streetcar. I saw many buildings and many windows, with many eyes peering out. I saw many trees. The streetcar was moving, the buildings were moving, and the trees were moving. Everything around the streetcar was moving as it moved. The streetcar came back to where they'd put the cap on my head. My grandfather took me up eagerly. He put me in a car, and we went to Damur. Damur was smaller, and more beautiful than Beirut because the sea there was grander. But it didn't have a streetcar. *Take me to the streetcar!* So they took me to the streetcar. I don't remember anything of Damur except the sea and the banana plantations. How big the banana leaves were! How big they were! And the red flowers climbing the walls of the houses.

When I came back to Beirut ten years ago, the first thing I did was stop a taxi and say to the driver: "Take me to Damur." I had come from Cairo and was searching for the small footsteps of a boy who had taken steps larger than himself, not in keeping with his age and greater than his stride. What was I searching for? The footsteps, or the boy? Or for the folks who had crossed a rocky wilderness, only to reach that which they didn't find, just as Cavafy never found his Ithaca? The sea was in place, pushing against Damur to make it bigger. And I had grown up. I had become a poet searching for the boy that used to be in him, whom he had left behind some place and forgotten. The poet had grown older and didn't permit the forgotten boy to grow up. Here I had harvested my first impressions, and here I had learned the first lessons. Here the lady who owned the orchard had kissed me. And here I had stolen the first roses. Here my grandfather had waited for the return to be announced in the newspaper, but it never was.

We came from the villages of Galilee. We slept one night by the filthy Rmesh pool, next to pigs and cows. The following morning, we moved north. I picked mulberries in Tyre. Then our journey came to an end in Jizzine. I had never seen snow before.

Jizzine was a snow farm, and it had a waterfall. I had never seen a waterfall before. And I had never known that apples hung from branches; I used to think they grew in boxes. We took small bamboo baskets and picked apples from the trees. *I want this one. I want that one.* I washed them in streams flowing down from the foot of the mountain into channels between small houses crowned with red tiles. In winter we couldn't bear the biting cold of the wind, so we moved to Damur. The sunset stole time from time itself. The sea writhed like the bodies of women in love until it raised its cry in the night and for the night.

The boy went back to his family *there,* in the distance, in a distance he did not find there in the distance. My grandfather died with his gaze fixed on a land imprisoned behind a fence. A land whose skin they had changed from wheat, sesame, maize, watermelons, and honeydews to tough apples. My grandfather died counting sunsets, seasons, and heartbeats on the fingers of his withered hands. He dropped like a fruit forbidden a branch to lean its age against. They destroyed his heart. He wearied of waiting here, in Damur. He said goodbye to friends, water pipe, and children and took me and went back to find what was no longer his to find *there. Here* the number of aliens increased, and refugee camps got bigger.[27] A war went by, then two, three,

27. About the refugees, David Gilmour, in *Dispossessed: The Ordeal of the Palestinians* (London: Sphere Books, 1982), p. 74, says:

> The exact number of refugees was never accurately established. The UN Economic Survey Mission report put the total at 726,000; the Refugee Office of the UN Palestine Conciliation Commission placed it at 900,000. The answer is probably somewhere in between. By the winter of 1948, therefore, when the fighting was over, perhaps 800,000 Palestinians had become homeless. . . . They expected to remain refugees for weeks, at worst months, and that afterwards they would be allowed home.

Smith, in *Palestine and the Israeli Conflict,* p. 154, describes the situation of the refugees at about the time referred to in the text as follows:

and four. The homeland got farther and farther away, and the children got farther and farther from mother's milk after they had tasted the milk of UNRWA. So they bought guns to get closer to a homeland flying out of their reach. They brought their identity back into being, re-created the homeland, and followed their path, only to have it blocked by the guardians of civil wars. They defended their steps, but then path parted from path, the orphan lived in the skin of the orphan, and one refugee camp went into another.

| | | | | | |

I cannot carve my name on a rock in Damur, even if it has been used as cover by snipers with designs on my life. I cannot. No, I cannot. Therefore, get this photographer away from the face of the rock. Keep this kind of talk away from a sea still in place. I cannot raise the banner of our martyrs from the shoulders of a corpse hanging from the top of a banana tree. No, I cannot. "War is war" is not my language. I will not read poetry in Damur. "What's to be done against that which cuts off one refugee camp from another?" is not my question. I have no interest whatever in carving my name on a rock in Damur because I'm searching for a boy here, not for a homeland.[28]

Palestinian Arabs living outside their former homeland, now refugees, encountered official sympathy and unofficial suspicion that led to their isolation in most of the countries where they settled. The bulk of the Palestinian Arabs in exile, over 500,000 in 1956, resided in Jordan. . . . Nearly 200,000 were crammed into the Gaza Strip, under Egyptian rule, where their movement was restricted. The nearly 100,000 refugees in Lebanon in 1956 had not been granted citizenship because the Maronite Christian ruling elite feared the addition of so many Muslims to the population.

28. After the devastation of Tel Zaatar refugee camp (see note 11), the coastal city of Damur fell to the Palestinian forces. The poet in this section

| | | | | | | |

In the rubble of Damur sons of martyrs and survivors from Tel Zaatar found yet another refuge in the chain of moving shelters. They brought their fatigue, disappointment, and the parts of their bodies the knives had forgotten to disjoin and came to Damur. They came in search of a place to sleep, on a square meter open to wind and patriotic songs. But what the primitive daggers forgot to do is being done by fighter planes, which haven't stopped shelling this human continuity. Where's all this leading? Where? From massacre to slaughter have my people been led, and still they bring forth offspring in debris-filled stopping places, flash victory signs, and prepare wedding feasts.

Does a bomb have grandchildren? Us.

Does a piece of shrapnel have grandparents? Us.

For ten years I've been living in Beirut in cement transiency. I try to unravel Beirut, and I become more and more ignorant of myself. Is it a city or a mask? A place of exile or a song? How quickly it ends! And how quickly it begins! The reverse is also true.

In other cities, memory can resort to a piece of paper. You may sit waiting for something, in a white void, and a passing idea may descend on you. You catch it, lest it escape, and as days roll and you come upon it again, you recognize its source and thank the city that gave you this present. But in Beirut you

---

severely criticizes the justifications for the occupation of Damur ("War is war"), what took place there (leaders having their photographs taken), and the atrocities that were committed (corpses dangling from banana trees).

flow away and scatter. The only container is water itself. Memory assumes the shape of the city's chaos and takes up a speech that makes you forget words that went before.

Rarely do you notice Beirut is beautiful.

Rarely in Beirut do you distinguish between content and form.

It's not old, and it's not new.

When they ask, "Do you love it?" you're surprised by the question and ask yourself, "Why didn't I pay attention? Do I love it?" Then you search for an emotion appropriate to it, and you ache with dizziness or stupor. Rarely do you need to be reassured you're in Beirut: you're in it with no need of evidence, and it's in you with no need for proof. And you remember that in Cairo this question would have driven you to the balcony to check whether the Nile was still there. If you saw the Nile, then you were in Cairo. But here, it's the sound of bullets that tells you you're in Beirut. The sound of bullets and the shriek of the slogans on the walls.

Is it a city or a refugee camp of Arab streets laid out with no plan? Or is it something else altogether? A condition, a thought, a change in state, a flower born from a text, or a young woman who unsettles the imagination.

Is it for this reason no one has been able to compose a song for Beirut?

How easy she seems!

Yet how she resists the joining together of words, even those with similar meter and rhyme: Beirut, *yaqoot, taboot*—"Beirut, sapphire, coffin!"

Or is it because she offers herself to a casual passerby, who then feels she's his private delight? Only its people and those with forgotten names are deprived of the wonder that comes upon others.

I don't know Beirut, and I don't know if I love or don't love it.

For the political refugee, there's a chair that can't be changed or replaced. Or, to put it more accurately, for the chair there's a political refugee whom it can't change.

For the refugee merchant there's an opportunity to discover that the winds of the fifties, which promised something to the Arab poor, will not blow this way again.

For the writer whose country is too confining, or who has grown weary of it, there's the freedom to believe he's free without knowing on which front he's fighting.

For the ex-poet there's the possibility of getting hold of a pistol, a guard, and money, thereby turning into a gang leader, assassinating a critic here and bribing another there.

For the traditional young woman there's the possibility of making her veil disappear into her handbag on the boarding ramp of an airliner, then disappearing into a hotel room with her lover.

It is for the smuggler to smuggle.

And for the poor to grow poorer.

Every visitor to Beirut finds his own special city, and we don't know—no one does—to what extent all these cities make up the city of Beirut, over which weepers are not weeping because it is over their memories and private interests they are weeping.

Perhaps in this manner—the manner in which Arabs came searching for something missing in their own countries—this meeting place of contraries was turned into an obscure naming, or a lung which a mixture of people, killers and victims among them, could use to breathe. This is what made of Beirut a song celebrating the singular and distinctive, where not many lovers asked whether they were really living in Beirut or in their dreams.

As for Beirut, no one knows her. And no one is searching for her. And perhaps, perhaps, she's not there at all. It was only in war that everyone realized they didn't know her. And Beirut herself realized that she wasn't one city, one homeland, or the meeting point of neighboring countries; that the distance between one window and another facing it could be greater than that between us and Washington; and that internecine fighting between one street and another parallel to it could be more intense than that between a Zionist and an Arab nationalist.

Only in war did the fighters realize that the peace of Beirut with Beirut was impossible.

And only in truce did fighters and observers realize this war was endless, and that victory—outside the balance of defeat—was impossible.

Perhaps everyone realized there was no Beirut in Beirut: for this lady sitting on a stone is like a sunflower that follows what doesn't belong to her, dragging lovers and enemies alike around a cycle of false appearances, sometimes with or against them, and other times not with or against them.

It is the form for a form that hasn't yet formed, because war within it—I mean around it—is now won, now lost. Because in it the constant is the variable and the permanent, the transitory.

Or take a wave. Set it on the rock at Raouche and break it down. All you'll find will be your hands sinking into a magical game with no beginning or end.

Question: Is it a mirror?

Answer: To the extent that a wave is fit to be a rock.

Question: Is it a road?

Answer: To the extent that a poem can be a street.

Question: Does it tell lies?

Answer: When one believes what can't be believed.

During the long war one could make her out clearly. It seemed to me then that beyond the blood and the fire, these faces, like those reflected in a mirror, would see what they had not seen before and change the source of their reflection. It seemed to me Beirut could be an island in the middle of the water or the desert. That the tribes forming a ring around the dance of fire would shift allegiance from tribal lineage to homeland. That the idea of homeland would become part of the idea of nation, and that the nation would discover the self-evident condition of its existence, such as knowing who or where the enemy is. It seemed to me that these martyrs, this new language, and this great pile of ashes would create for us a sign at least. It seemed the transformation had begun, that the shell of regionalism had been broken and the pearl, the essence, had shown itself.

So it seemed to me then.

So it seemed to me.

| | | | | | |

Yet the bird that rose from the blood of Beirut and its promises started to ask: "Am I in open space or in a cage?"

I am passing through Beirut and see a cage made of wing feathers. It is the spring of 1980. My lyrics provoke ridicule. I've become the only stranger.

—Have I made mistakes?

—Yes, many.

—Get out of here!

—Is the war over?

—All the conquerors are gone, and the homeland has been born anew.

—Where shall I return?

—To your country.

—Where is my country?

—Within the Arab nation.

—And Palestine?

—Peace swallowed her.

I've become the only stranger. What will I do in Paris? *What you do in Beirut.* How long will I stay in London? *As long as you stay in Beirut.*

Tell me: What happened to Beirut?

He says: It became strong.

I ask: Has Arabism won her, or . . . ?

He says: Neither this nor that. The winds blowing in the region have won her, because she wasn't capable of being an island in water or an oasis in the desert. Go back to where you came from because the street here rejects you.

And I've become the only stranger.

How often have I held back my complaint: Why should the Lebanese homeland be incompatible with Palestine? Why should the Egyptian loaf be incompatible with Palestine?

Why should the Syrian roof be incompatible with Palestine?
Why should Palestine be incompatible with Palestine?

How I feel like a stranger here, in the spring of 1980! The
wind warns, the airport road warns, and the sea warns of some-
thing. And I've become the only stranger.

On the walls, official placards nibble away yet more photo-
graphs of martyrs and more of the words that held the homeland
together on the signposts of the new highway. Beirut passed this
way. I searched for the girl from the south who ate her official
identity card and found her practicing the official anthem and
waiting for the armored vehicle that will bring her to the feast.

A homeland indeed.

Beirut crowned with the contrivances of beauty, oratory,
and protocol against which Beirut rebelled when it passed this
way. A return to the disparities that lit up the four-year war is
now the common aspiration. Beirut is once again the homeland
of a language against which it rebelled. Why not? Why not? Why
not? And now, all of a sudden, peace reigns in the south, except
for some areas tied to Palestine with a thread of blood. Peace
would reign in the south, if not for Palestine.

I see Beirut crying over the south. I mean, I see intellectuals
and officials crying over the south. Suddenly they remember
Beirut is the capital of Lebanon, and the south belongs to Leba-
non. And I remember how they used to forget the south when
jets were roasting it. Before the establishment of Haddad Land
they used to sit in cafés and bars drinking beer and lamenting
the suffering in Biafra.[29] In those days the concept of homeland

---

29. "Haddad Land" refers to an area in the south of Lebanon that Israel
set up under the control of Major Saad Haddad, a dissident Lebanese army

annoyed the Israelis, who acknowledge no borders for a home-
land. Then, homeland meant duty, and duty meant protecting
the south from Israeli tanks and jets. Then, the concept of
homeland was not in need of a home.

—What's new, my friend?

—Luxurious buildings are full of refugees from the south,
and refugees pay no rent.

—What's new, my friend?

New pain drives the old pain away, and new problems chase
away the old. And you are the only stranger.

These questions arouse the scorn of a Beirut looking for a
new equilibrium to replace the old and an old homeland to re-
place the new. The currents search for the seashells from which
they came, and one has the right to blame them only to the
extent one has the right to believe what one believes. They claim
the war of promises is over and the building of state authority
has begun. Yet the mirror no longer reflects anything but what's
in front of it.

And this very sky is a cage.

---

officer, as its so-called security zone following its withdrawal from Lebanon after
the 1978 invasion.

The subsequent reference to the refugees from the south in the text is
explained by that invasion, which, David Gilmour says (*Lebanon: The Fractured
Country*, p. 149), created a "huge number of refugees, the United Nations calcu-
lating that [it] made a quarter of a million people homeless. Many of these were
Shi'ites who had been made homeless twice already—once by Israeli raids in the
early seventies which had forced them to move to Beirut, and again when the
civil war in the capital had persuaded them that it was safer to return to their
original homes."

| | | | | | |

Beyond all that, you must be white; for there is something more precious than freedom and life itself. What is it?

Whiteness.

> Naturalists tell us that the ermine is a little animal with a fur of extreme whiteness and that when hunters wish to catch it they use this trick: they find the places it usually passes and frequents and stop them up with mud; and then, starting their quarry, they drive it that way. Now, when the ermine reaches the mud, it stands still and lets itself be seized and caught rather than pass through the dirt, and soil and lose its whiteness, which it values more than its life and liberty.[30]

| | | | | | |

Does a bomb have grandchildren? Us.

Does a piece of shrapnel have grandparents? Us.

And the silence, the silence of the spectators, has turned into boredom. *When will the hero crack? When will he crack, and break the alternation of the amazing and the ordinary?* Heroism invites boredom when the scene goes on too long and initial excitement fades. Hasn't the issue of this heroism itself been pushed until it has become a source of boredom in the context of a life that longs only for the ordinary, free of causes and loud cheers? Pushed to the point of boredom so that Arab leaders, faced with this heroism, can proclaim the causes of misery:

---

30.   Cervantes, *Don Quixote*, "The Tale of Foolish Curiosity," trans. J. M. Cohen (Harmondsworth, Middlesex: Penguin Books, 1977), p. 290.

Palestine is responsible for the disappearance of wheat from the fields; for the flourishing of an architecture whose crowning gems are prisons; and for the transformation of agriculture into an industry that produces nothing but the bellies of a new class, newly rich and weighed down by the worries of individual consumption, burdening the state with debts the ordinary citizen would need two lifetimes to pay back.

Egypt has tried this state of bliss. The mirage of peace promised that bread would be liberated from the Palestine tax, promised the safe return of martyrs to their families and a more satisfying meal of fava beans. Luxuries flourished, the years of betrothal stretched to an unnamed time when the impossible search for a marriage nest would be over, and the hungry got hungrier. And Sadat put anyone who asked, "What are we getting in return for this peace?" in prison, until a youth from the ranks of his own guards came forth to shoot down pharaoh, peace, and the mirage itself.

And the others? They learned their lesson, cast away Sadat's passion for the orator's platform, and ushered in, patiently and methodically, the peace of the fait accompli, which required binding the Arab stomach to satisfactory American conditions. They turned the Arab stomach into a hostage and declared war, with weapons and with silence, against the subject of heroism. And, a little embarrassed, they waited for the Israelis to burn down, on behalf of all, the stage for this heroism and the platform for this alternate form of oratory. Heroism also invites boredom. *Enough!* And they differed on how to market this boredom. Some advocated waiting for a future time, when the balance of forces would turn in our favor by means of a magic wand from outside that would guarantee us the right to dictate conditions for war or peace. Others, wanting to hasten the end, advised us to leave on American ships immediately and unconditionally. Still others wanted to bring on the end by urging us to commit collective suicide so they could take over our theater as well as their own.

Enough! How long are they going to resist? Either they die or get out of Beirut. How long are they going to spoil Arab evenings with corpses that interrupt the sequence of American television series? How long are they going to carry on the fight when it's the height of the season for vacations, the World Cup, and the raising of frogs? Let them clear the way before our passions and our shame! Let this comedy come to an end! Their wise men, dignified by decorous sympathy, offer an even more interesting tableau on the stage of boredom: "It's time for them to realize there's no hope. No hope from the Arabs—a nation that doesn't deserve to live! A nation in the image of its leaders! This is a losing battle, and they might as well save their blood for another day."

A silence crowned with all that empties history of toasts. Ornamental horses on battlefields used to seasons of conquest. An unchanging speech that longs for the alienation of words from what lies behind them. An unchanging speech that compounds the rust that has been accumulating on language since the orator mounted the throne of the speaker's platform. An unchanging speech delivered by those divided and fighting among themselves over a speech. Does a city this size and with so much chaos have the right to grant time itself another name? Does it have the right to scribble over a finished painting? Does it have the right to approach the fence of a well-fenced-in conflict and set down different rules for the neighbors of the enemy? This is their name and their title: "the neighbors of the enemy."

In that case, "Death to Beirut!" is the address of the death of this last street that lies outside the geometry of obedience.

They got bored. Bored. The wait has gone on too long for the fall of the last meaning that hangs like ripe fruit from the dried-up palm tree of the Arabs—dangles for its heirs to bury rather than to gather and store. *When will they stop this madness? When will they go away? When will they fade into the obscurity of sand? When will they fall as we have fallen, but with a healthy difference? We trip over thrones, moving from resounding defeat directly to the throne while they trip over a coffin, going from heroism to the coffin.*

In the quiver of boredom there's something resembling wisdom: we, we are the ones to determine the place of the battle and its outcome. And we won't use this weapon except during times of hardship. Who knows what times of hardship are like, and where hardship is to be found in this luxurious leisure? They themselves know better than we do. It may come from a quarter or a street that rises up in anger. But what will anger the people? We've become addicted to scoffing at their leaders while always forgiving their indifference, hoping to cure hope itself of an incurable disease.

Is there no one on this continent who knows how to say no? Is there no one? No one.

The ministers of defense amused themselves with champagne bubbles, in the company of the killers, when news arrived announcing the tightening of the siege around Tel Zaatar. How are they amusing themselves now, with the siege around Beirut tightening? We saw them in photographs around their swimming pools: isn't the month of August hot? And we saw the fatigue of their heavily armed guards gathering their masters' smiles as they oozed down to their knees, in an attempt to return them safely to their open mouths. Safe from the gaze of passersby and from the siege of Beirut.

But I am not angered, as others are, by the tumultuous Arab demonstrations which erupt in protest over a biased referee decision in a soccer match—not because soccer fires enthusiasm better than this prolonged holding out in Beirut, but because that which has been repressed in Arab breasts, springing from various sources, has found a permitted point of explosion.[31] In soccer they find an opportunity to express chronic anger in a war that doesn't materially threaten the nation—a conflict of morale which in forty-five minutes must end in a truce, when those fighting on opposite sides (having filled their armory with needed morale and public support) rearrange their ranks, replan lines of defense and attack, and resume the fight under the supervision of international forces that forbid the use of weapons proscribed by the world community. This limited war, under strict control on the battlefield and elsewhere, then ends without spilling over the boundaries of either country—except in rare cases, as happened between El Salvador and Honduras. But in that case the Security Council, maintaining a delicate international balance, issued a resolution that could be enforced.

And because I love soccer, the contrast doesn't anger me as it does others. The siege of Beirut did not stir up a single Arab demonstration, while soccer matches have given rise to many during the siege. Why should that not be the case? Soccer is the

31. In 1982, during the siege of Beirut, the Algerian soccer team reached the semifinals of the World Cup but lost to Germany. The defeat, attributed to a biased decision of a referee, led to massive demonstrations in some Arab capitals.

field of expression permitted by secret understanding between ruler and ruled in the prison cell of Arab democracy, which threatens to destroy guards along with prisoners. The game represents a breathing space, allowing a splintered homeland an opportunity to join together around something shared, a consensus in which, for each team, the boundary lines and the conditions of the relationship are clearly defined, whatever cunning hints may slip through and whatever repressed meanings spectators may project upon the game. A homeland, or a manifestation of its spirit, defends its dignity or its lead against the Other, without disturbing the internal arrangement of forces. The spectators take on the roles denied them in politics, giving them shape and projecting them onto the intelligence of muscles and the maneuvers of the players in the movement toward one end—scoring a goal.

But the leader, in appointing himself spokesman for the spirit of the nation, sees victory as the outcome of his wise rule and his ability to engage the will and energies of the people. Perhaps it's he, not the player, who's more adept at interpreting events, for he's the owner of the nation and its shepherd, who spends from his own pocket to encourage sports. Yet the situation is reversed when the result deviates from the desired and expected—when the player/homeland is defeated before the Other. In that case, the leader denies responsibility for defeat, blaming it on the teams, or on tradition, or on the coach, or on the bad luck of the players/fighters, or on the bias of external forces, represented by the referee.

No; defeat has more than one father. In politics, it hasn't been the modern Arab tradition to punish the leader for a defeat. He *will* go to the masses for sympathy, and they will console him by begging him to stay on the throne to outwit the enemy. For what does the enemy want but to bring down the leader and rescue us from the blessing of his presence? Let us therefore defeat the enemy and win a victory over ourselves as well by keeping the defeated leader as our executioner.[32]

In soccer, on the other hand, the situation is different. The public does have the power to express its anger against the players, the coach, and the foreign referee. *The players have betrayed the spirit of the nation, the coach has set a bad game plan, and the referee was biased.* As for the leader, he will not in any case be blamed for the defeat, because he is busy with other, more important, matters. The angry crowd will very likely take to the streets, raise his picture very, very high, and slip under it for some freedom of expression. It can curse the West all it wants, as well as make gestures for internal consumption. This is all we have left of freedom. Are we then to let go of it so easily? This is all we have left of pleasure; let us therefore applaud these signs of well-being! The nation is in good health as long as it is capable of such enthusiasm. The soccer game tells us that much. It tells us that collective emotion has not atrophied, that it is still possible to rouse the street for a game that doesn't give rise to boredom. Did not Palestine, in what has passed of our present, occupy this very position, generating emotion and patriotic fer-

32. The reference in this paragraph may be to Gamal Abdel Nasser, whose ideas concerning Arab unity and a secular Arab nationalism Darwish praises elsewhere in the book. Nasser resigned after the 1967 defeat, but the masses came out in huge demonstrations in his support. Later, it was bruited about (as Darwish hints here) that the Arabs did not really lose the war, because the aim of the Israelis had been to bring down President Nasser, and since Nasser hadn't fallen, the war was not really lost.

vor? Hasn't everything been done in her name, on her behalf, and for her sake?

It used to be that whatever touched Palestine would touch the Arab public with sadness, tumult, and rage; that the people would bring down a leader for any violence done to this collective heart. But now the rulers are in a race to bribe the people and force them into giving up this consensus. The Arab military establishment has openly set itself against Palestinian action and the Palestinian idea, blaming them for the misery of the Arab nation and its slavishness. *If it were not for Palestine, the imagined and imaginary, the impossible to attain, the one arriving early for a delayed appointment and moving too quickly for Arab unity—if it were not for Palestine, we would now have more freedom, and greater luxury and comfort.* Thus does official Arab speech broadcast rumors that inspire boredom. But the people know how to maneuver, how to read events, and how to interpret figurative language. Prisons are not a condition for the liberation of Palestine. And the slogan "No voice can rise above the voice of the battle!" has brought forth only one meaning: no Palestine, no battle, and no voice. Long live the whip! Therefore, the issue of bread and freedom has infiltrated the question of liberation, raised with impunity until Arab rulers betrayed their ambiguous game by banning Palestine outright, keeping it outside the national arena, and removing the question of social conditions from the discourse of the Arab nation.

Soccer provides the outlet previously provided by Palestine. Let the street rise in anger then, and let it smuggle its repressed question into a game that doesn't inspire boredom or give the ruler the opportunity to close the gates of the playing field.

A silence crowned with the illusions of those who till now have been able to divide all sides and all colors into two.

A silence crowned with the illusions of those still able to await deliverance.

A silence gilded with hope awaited from outside. The silence of those who guide the rhetoric of revolution to sources outside itself—a carefully controlled and deeply rooted rhetoric of subservience that exchanges the roles of street and capital and accuses other capitals in the name of the street, while exempting its own capital (the very limit of its knowledge). A rhetoric that assigns one capital to absolute evil and another to absolute good, substituting, any time it needs to, another capital for its own without letting up on the revolutionary gush that is synonymous with capitals.

Let there be capitals! Let there be capitals!

| | | | | | | |

Why is the idol shaking so? Why does it shake?

It will say the opposite of what it is. It will mouth the opposite of the silence in which it is wrapped.

It will carry on, repeating the lesson of the beginning.

It will glorify the fact that history, with its massacres and torture, has fulfilled its predictions. *Didn't I tell you?*

But you haven't said anything, Sir Idol.

He slips into the government, to be in the opposition; and he slips into the opposition to become the government. He fights against authority by means of another authority. And he's such an absolute follower, he has no followers of this own.

This is your hour, Sir Idol. Say something to keep yourself an idol forever.

He'll say something else after anything else.

He'll say he didn't agree to pull out of Beirut.

He'll say he told us so.

But he hasn't said anything.

Why am I seeing the Idol for the tenth time? Why am I seeing the Idol?[33]

| | | | | | | |

A silence made of gold. A silence made of malicious pleasure. That is why I was so impressed by Arab anger with the "racist Western conspiracy" against the newborn Arab participation in the World Cup. It was the only pointer to the existence of something outside our rocket fences, the only indicator that the nation wasn't going to permit foreigners to bruise its spirit. It was an ironic reply to the call by Arab foreign ministers for a meeting in Tunis to look into "the possibility" of holding an Arab summit conference to discuss the Israeli conquest. It was also an ironic reply to the state of Lebanon for not having protested against this conquest, limiting itself to the role of mediator between the American special envoy and the Palestinian leadership. We therefore asked, "Why should the summit masters of the Arab abyss play with fire and get their garlic and onions burned, and their fingers in the process?" Is there not enough time for more conquest, more swallowing of land and people? It's only been a month since the invasion began. In the history of immortal Arab rule a single month is no more than a fleeting moment, which is not long enough even to formulate the reply

33. The Idol is apparently a reference to a high-ranking person in the Palestinian leadership.

of the Arab states to the falsehoods of the envoy sent to them, who said, "There is an Arab and international consensus to eliminate the Palestinian Movement." *Get lost!* Why then should the Arab states be in such a hurry ("Haste," as the proverb has it, "is from the cursed, whose father is the devil") for their foreign ministers to spend some difficult hours in Tunis arguing over the aims and extent of the Israeli attack? *Is this attack directed against Palestinians and Lebanese only, or is it also against all Arabs? Will it go beyond announced Israeli aims?*

And they will also debate the definition of oil. Is it a commodity, or a political weapon? Once again, they feel bored because the expected news hasn't been announced. The Movement is not yet dead, and there is still enough fuel and arms in Israeli warehouses to finish off fifty thousand Lebanese and Palestinian children. There is still enough conventional military hardware in American warehouses to annihilate all cities. And there is still enough water, canned goods, and oxygen left in Beirut to keep the Movement going. And there is still enough space in the open Arab skies for more passes by Israeli bombers. And there is still enough room in the Mediterranean for more submarines, aircraft carriers, and international treaties. And there are still many civilian targets in Beirut that have not been hit. Why therefore the hurry? Why the hurry?

And we too love soccer. We too have a right to love the game, and a right to see the match. Why not? Why shouldn't we put aside the routines of death for a moment? In one of the bomb shelters we were able to draw electrical power from a car battery and, watching Paolo Rossi, in no time at all were feeling what little happiness there was to be felt. You never see him anywhere on the playing field except where he has to be. A thin devil of a man who can't be seen except after the goal is scored, exactly like a jet fighter, invisible until the explosion of its target. And where Paolo Rossi is, there the goal will be and the cheers. Then he will disappear or fade away, only to open paths in the air for his feet, busy concocting opportunities and ripening them, then sending them off to the summit of realized desire. One doesn't know if he's playing soccer or playing the game of love with the net. The net resists, and he tempts it, luring it with Italian chivalry and elegance on a hot Spanish playing field. He tempts it with the slipping and sliding movements of a cat aroused by cries of desire. And in full sight of those guarding its chastity, who afterwards reseal its virginity with a membrane of ten men, Paolo Rossi will come forward, totally passionate, to penetrate with a muscle made of air a net that surrenders to a beautiful ravishment, relaxed, willing to be taken, and no longer able to resist.

Soccer.

What is this magical madness that can declare a truce for the sake of an innocent pleasure? What is this madness that can lighten the savagery of war and turn rockets into annoying flies? And what is this madness that suspends fear for an hour and a half, coursing through body and soul more rapturously, even, than poetry, wine, or the first encounter with an unknown woman?

During the siege a soccer match brought about a miracle, inspiring movement in a street we had thought dead of fear and boredom.

I didn't rejoice over the demonstrations in Tel Aviv, which continues to rob us of all our roles. From them the killer and the victim, from them the pain, and the cry; the sword, and the rose; the victory, and the defeat. I didn't rejoice because their intent was to banish the heroes from the stage. They had grown accustomed to easy wars and easy victories. The rivalry between the two large political parties facilitated the opening of the streets of Tel Aviv for tens of thousands of demonstrators. And the number of their casualties roused them to the extent that a high-ranking officer resigned. I listened to their radio but never understood the secret behind their crying. The victor was defeated from within. The victor was afraid to lose his identity as victim. No one else had the right to realize this achievement—to become the victim—because the reversal of roles would upset a scale of justice made of sand. For our sake they shouted, for our sake they cried; but they won wars for their own worth's sake.

Is there anything more cruel than this absence: that you should not be the one to celebrate your victory or the one to lament your defeat? That you should stay offstage and not make an entrance except as a subject for others to take up and interpret. "If you have the will, then it's not a myth"—that is Theodore Herzl's Zionist slogan calling for the establishment of a "homeland for a people without a land on a land without a people." But during the siege of Beirut, which bore witness to the existence of a people with a land confronting invaders who had robbed them of it, Nathan Zach, a modern Hebrew poet, with brilliant irony, modified Herzl's slogan: "Israel's victory does not disappoint, but it will not last long enough to fail." Scores of Hebrew poems, but no Arabic poems, address the siege of Beirut and protest the massacre. From them the sin, and from them the forgiveness. From them the killing, and the tears. From them the massacres, and the justice of the courts.

| | | | | | |

Then came a year . . .

That year, the Franks took Jerusalem and killed more than sixty thousand Muslims. They broke into homes, wreaking havoc wherever they went. From the Dome of the Rock they took forty-two silver chandeliers, each weighing more than three thousand six hundred dirhams. And they took a silver cauldron weighing forty Damascene rotls, as well as twenty-three gold lamps. Then the people ran away, fleeing Syria for Iraq, asking for assistance against the Franks from the supreme ruler, the caliph. When people heard of these grave matters, they were struck with terror and cried out. Then the caliph delegated the theologians to go about in the land and urge the kings to the fight. Thus, Ibn Uqail and many another of the foremost theologians went about among the people, but it was no use. We are God's, and to Him we shall return. Concerning this topic, Abu al-Mudhaffar al-Abyouri wrote: "The worst weapon a man can wield is a tear / When with sharp swords the fire of war is lit."

That year, Sultan Muhammad Ben Melkshah went to Rai and there found the Lady Zubaida, mother of his brother Barkyariq, and ordered that she be strangled. Her age then was forty-two years.

That year, Sultan Melkshah sent a letter to al-Hassan Ibn Sabbah, a preacher of esoteric doctrine. Citing the judgments of the jurists, he threatened him, forbidding his form of belief. And when he read the letter in the presence of the messenger, he said to the youths around him: "I want to send one of you with him to his master." Their heads shot up expectantly. Then he said to one of them,

"Kill yourself"; and that one brought out a knife, plunged it into his own throat, and fell dead. Then he said to another, "Throw yourself from here." And that one threw himself from the top of the citadel down into the trench, and his body was crushed. Then he said to the messenger, "This is your answer."

That year, the Franks took many forts, including Caesarea and Sarrouj, and the king of the Franks, Kandar—he was the one who conquered Jerusalem—marched to Acre and put it under siege.

That year, a certain man from around Nahawand claimed he was a prophet and named four of his friends after the first four caliphs.

That year, a blind girl appeared who could reveal people's secrets and their innermost wishes and desires. The people went to great extremes to confound her and find out her secret, but they never succeeded. They asked about rings with seals carved in a mirror image, difficult to decipher. They asked about different kinds of gems, and people's qualities. And they asked about what might be found inside bird traps—such as wax, different kinds of clay, and cloth—and she answered all questions equally well. One of them even put his hand on his member and asked what it was. "Let him carry it home to his wife and family," she said.

That year, Khatoun, daughter of King Melkshah and wife of the caliph, came to Baghdad and stayed at the house of her brother, Sultan Muhammad. Her trousseau was brought on the backs of two hundred and sixty-two camels and twenty-seven mules. And the Franks conquered many cities, including Sidon and others.

That year, they fought back in Syria and regained many

forts from the Franks. And when they entered Damascus, the emir Mowdood, prince of Mosul, came into its mosque to pray. He was approached by a believer in esoteric doctrine dressed like a beggar, who begged from him. The emir wanted to give him something, but the man approached and stabbed him in the heart and he died instantly.

That year, a letter arrived from the Franks that said, "A nation that kills its leader in the house of worship on the day of its feast—it is only proper that God should destroy it."

That year, the caliph decided to circumcise his brother's children. They were twelve boys, and Baghdad was decorated in a manner never seen before.

That year, in the land of Mosul a great rain fell, but some of it was like a blazing fire that burned many houses. And in Baghdad, flying scorpions with two stingers appeared, and the people were sorely frightened.

That year, a man was found sodomizing a boy and was thrown down from the top of a minaret. The Franks took many forts in the Andalusian peninsula. King Nour al-Din Ibn Mahmoud Zanki took back many forts on the coast from the Franks. And Saif al-Din Ghazi married the daughter of Sahib Mardin Husam al-Din Tamartash Ben Artaq, after having put him under siege. They sealed the peace with the marriage. The girl was taken to Mosul two years later but found her husband on his deathbed. He died without consummating the marriage. After his death, his brother Qutb Ben Mowdood took over, and he married the girl.

That year, a rain fell in Yemen that was all blood, and it dyed people's clothes.

That year, a rooster laid one egg, a falcon laid two, and an ostrich laid an egg without having been with a male. There was also a great battle between Nour al-Din al-Shaheed and the Franks, and he defeated them and killed many of them.

That year, there was a great wind with a fire after the evening prayer, and the people became worried that the final hour had come. There was an earthquake, and the water of the River Tigris turned red. And in the land of Wasit blood appeared, but its origin was unknown. And the Franks took Asqalan.

That year, the cost of living rose precipitously in Khorasan, and people ate even insects. One of them slaughtered an Alawite man, cooked him, and sold him in the market. When what he had done became known, he was killed for it.

That year, huge hailstones fell in Iraq, each weighing nearly five rotles. Some weighed nine rotles by the Baghdadi scale. The graves caved in, and the dead floated on the water. And the king of the Franks came marching on Damascus with many legions, but God turned him back empty-handed. That year also, Afif al-Nasikh said, "I saw someone in a dream, and he said: 'If three *F*'s were to come together, then Caliph al-Muqtafi would die'—the intended meaning here is five hundred and fifty-five."

That year, Saladin wrote the various emirs, blaming them for drawing up truces with the Franks and paying them money in tribute even though they were fewer and less courageous. He informed them of his intention to come to Syria to protect it from the Franks, but they answered him in a coarse and ugly manner, and he paid them no heed.

That year, the honorable qadi, al-Fadhil, also sent the emirs a letter with the preacher Shams al-Din on behalf of the Sultan—an extraordinary letter, eloquent and beautiful in tone—in which he said, "Let it be known to you that we were the ones who held fire in our palms, while others benefited from the light. We were the ones who found water, while others took their supply. And we received the arrows in our throats, while others fell back on pretense." But when they received the letter, they wrote a rude answer.

That year, the king of the English sent a letter to Saladin saying he had brought birds of prey with him from abroad, but they were in very weak condition. He asked for some chickens and other fowl so that his birds could regain their strength. Saladin understood that he was asking for these things to assuage his own hunger. So he generously sent him a large quantity. Then the English king asked for fruits and ice, which Saladin also supplied. But this kindness did no good, for as soon as he recovered, he came back even more fiercely than before. The siege of Acre intensified; it went on night and day. The inhabitants of the city sent word to the sultan that if nothing was done by the morrow they were going to ask for a truce and for security from the Franks. The sultan found that difficult to take.

That year, a truce was signed to stop the war, after thirty years and six months. The Franks would keep what lands they held on the coast, and the Muslims would keep the hill country; the districts in between were to be divided half and half . . ."[34]

---

34. Ibn Kathir, *Al-bida:ya wa al-Niha:ya* (The Beginning and the End); my translation.

| | | | | | |

The Franks are void of all zeal and jealousy. One of them
may be walking along with his wife. He meets another
man who takes the wife by the hand and steps aside to con-
verse with her while the husband is standing on one side
waiting for his wife to conclude the conversation. If she lin-
gers too long for him, he leaves her alone with the conver-
sant and goes away.

Here is an illustration which I myself witnessed:

When I used to visit Nablus, I always took lodging with
a man named Mu'izz, whose home was a lodging house
for Moslems. The house had windows which opened to
the road, and there stood opposite to it on the other side
of the road a house belonging to a Frank who sold wine
for the merchants. He would take some wine in a bottle
and go around announcing it by shouting, "So and so, the
merchant, has just opened a cask full of this wine. He who
wants to buy some of it will find it in such and such a
place." . . . One day this Frank went home and found a
man with his wife in the same bed. He asked him, "What
could have made thee enter into my wife's room?" The
man replied, "I was tired, so I went in to rest." "But how,"
asked he, "didst thou get into my bed?" The other replied,
"I found a bed that was spread, so I slept in it." "But," said
he, "my wife was sleeping together with thee!" The other
replied, "Well, the bed is hers. How could I therefore have
prevented her from using her own bed?" "By the truth of
my religion," said the husband, "if thou shouldst do it
again, thou and I would have a quarrel." Such was for the
Frank the entire expression of his disapproval and the
limit of his jealousy.

Another illustration:

We had with us a bath-keeper named Salem, originally an inhabitant of al-Ma'arrah, who had charge of the bath of my father (may Allah's mercy rest upon his soul!). This man related the following story:

"I once opened a bath in al-Ma'arrah in order to earn my living. To this bath there came a Frankish knight. The Franks disapprove of girding a cover around one's waist while in the bath. So this Frank stretched out his arm and pulled off my cover from my waist and threw it away. He looked and saw that I had recently shaved off my pubes. So he shouted, 'Salem!' As I drew near him he stretched his hand over my pubes and said, 'Salem, good! By the truth of my religion, do the same for me.' Saying this, he lay on his back and I found that in that place the hair was like his beard. So I shaved it off. Then he passed his hand over the place and, finding it smooth, he said, 'Salem, by the truth of my religion, do the same to al-dama' (al-dama in their language means the lady), referring to his wife. He then said to a servant of his, 'Tell madame to come here.' Accordingly the servant went and brought her and made her enter the bath. She also lay on her back. The knight repeated, 'Do what thou has done to me.' So I shaved all that hair while her husband was sitting looking at me. At last he thanked me and handed me the pay for my service."

Consider now this great contradiction! They have neither jealousy nor zeal but they have great courage, although courage is nothing but the product of zeal and of ambition to be above ill repute.[35]

35. *An Arab-Syrian Gentleman and Warrior in the Period of the Crusades: Memoirs of Usamah Ibn-Munqidh* (Kita:b al-I?tiba:r), trans. Philip Hitti (Princeton, N.J.: Princeton University Press, 1987), pp. 164–66.

‖ ‖ ‖ ‖ ‖ ‖ ‖

The hours of the afternoon. Ashes made of steam and steam made of ashes. Metal is time's master, and nothing cuts one metal except another that carves a different history. The shelling leaves nothing alone, and there appears to be no end to this day. August is the cruelest month. August is the longest of months. And today is the cruelest day in August, and the longest. Is there no end to this day? I don't know what is happening on the outskirts of the city because the roar of metal has put a barrier between us and the deafening silence of our Arab brothers. A barrier between us and the silence of kings, presidents, and ministers of defense, who are busy not reading what they read. Nothing is left for us except the weapon of madness. To be, or not to be. To be, or to be. Not to be, or not to be. Nothing is left except madness.

> Block your blockade with madness
> Madness
> With madness
> And with madness
> They have gone, the ones you love. Gone.
> You will either have to be
> Or you will not be.

History whose shape and chroniclers are changing. A history that writes the shape of a river. Who, then, will write the history of the bottom, the history of the moss? Who will write the history of the enemy's birth from the brother, and the brother's entrance into the enemy?

What has made this snail appear in my face again? A snail

bearing the burden of its green saliva. A snail holding up a wall and preventing us from approaching another wall, watered with our blood, that it, the snail, may take over the throne. We, the ones suffering from indigestion with an excess of death for what's not ours, are even now defending what's not ours. And this road leading to the mountain is not for us. Nor is this orator's platform, which the snail will mount and use to fight for glory against other nations over a history not its own—a history stolen from the hero who needed a place to put down his heel. Why has the snail appeared in my face again today? Death to this day! Death to it!

I sit in a far corner, away from others and myself, thinking about a dream that came, born from another dream. *Are you still alive? When did it happen?* Will memory protect me from this threat? Will the lily of the past be able to break this bomb-studded sword? And why her? Why her? Why should the Lily of the Valley rise from the Song of Songs, when she has stopped sun and moon over the walls of Jericho, that the time of slaughter may be drawn out?

| | | | | | |

A time for childhood, and a time for lust. A body made for forgiveness; a body made for desires. The marble of speech melts to polish the praise of legs that split the graveyard into two gardens—one for the past, and one for the dream. The first lightning flashes in youthful bones.[36] How many women are you,

36. The text here collapses time and place into a moment of reverie, where the literal turns into the metaphorical, and vice versa. The graveyard is a reference to an actual graveyard through which the footpath between two villages in Upper Galilee passed during the poet's youth. Darwish's earliest mem-

you barefoot heavenly cluster? How many women are in you,
that I may plummet into the press of my spirit and be saved as
the moment is born? How many women are you, that time may
enter into time and come out a silken thread, singling me out
for the gallows of the blood? How many women are in you that
this moment may, on two feet—seals of heaven and hell—take
the shape of a history of prayer and lust? How many women are
you, that the history of this belly, kneaded from the fragrance of
jasmine and its color, lost between light and milk, may become
the story of battles waged to defend youth and one's forties?
How many women are you, that I may bring back a winter al-
ready past out of rain yet to fall, from whose drops I can collect
something that will feel like what I've known and thus be able
to compare one rapture with another? Were we really together,
lying on the wool of that land? When that which can be made
anew within us unites me with the thought that I'm with you, I
bring back what isn't squandered of a passion that shakes rooms.
I didn't say "I love you" because I didn't know if I loved you so
long as I kept hiding my blood under your skin and shedding
the honey of bees gone crazy in the capillaries of the holy sacra-
ment—the sacrament that so absorbed me that my body was in
a moment of continuous birth. And you didn't say "I love you"
because I wouldn't have believed that all women born on Mount
Gilead, in Sumer, and in the Valley of the Kings had come to-
gether for my sake tonight. How many women are in you, that
my dreams may cry a lament for what the nations have lost, a

_____

ory of an overwhelming sexual desire—when the "first lightning flashes in
youthful bones"—was that of seeing a woman's bare legs as she walked on
that path.

winter whose mother and goddess you deserve to be? In every beautiful woman there's a gift donated by the commandments of your feet to the earth, and an inheritance that doesn't cease supplying the forests with the hysteria of weeds. If only one of us hated the other so that love might fall in love! If only one of us would forget the other so that forgetfulness itself might be stricken with memory! And may one of us die before the other so that madness might be stricken with madness!

| | | | | | |

"Take me to Australia," she said. And I realized the time had come for us to get away from discord and war. "Take me to Australia"—because I couldn't reach Jerusalem. I had come out of the June War of 1967 with a determination that left me no peace. It was for armies to be defeated, the bee in my heart to stay steadfast, and the spirit to be victorious over me and my enemies. Chivalry and lyricism were blazing for me another trail that led up a mountain overlooking fields of history: horses' bones, armor full of holes, and weeds. From that lookout, the actual diminished and the wave no longer served as an address for the sea; I could thus protect myself and perhaps others from the turmoil of the moment by shifting from martyr to spectator.

But why am I remembering her in this hell, and at this hour of the afternoon? And in this air-raid shelter of a bar? Is it because the woman sitting across from me is reenacting the screaming scene? Or is it because a dream brought her out of my dream at dawn? I don't know, exactly as I don't know why I remember my mother, the first lesson in reading, my first girl under the pine tree, and the riddle of the shepherd's pipe that has chased me for twenty-five years. The circle returns to its starting point.

(*Each would kill the other outside the window.*) [37]

"Don't bite me like an apple; the whole night's still ours. Take me to Australia, where there's no one belonging to you or me, not even you and me."

She had put some logs on the fire, and the song about Suzanne taking you down to her place by the river was repeating the Song itself. The words were beautiful; and the voice was not so much singing as reading a poem that had nowhere to go. A human being alone in a wilderness. A human being who speaks to hold himself together, to protect himself from being alone, to point himself out to himself.

"When are you going to kiss me?"

"When I believe that I can believe these lips are open for me."

"For whom, then?"

"For a voice arriving from a distant planet. Do you know that your eyes can give night any color you wish?"

"Kiss me!"

Light rain outside the window, and embers inside.

"Why is it raining so much?"

"For you to stay inside me."

37. This line, repeated like a leitmotif every time the poet recollects his passion for his Israeli lover, the "Lily of the Valley," is taken from Darwish's poem "A Beautiful Woman in Sodom," which first appeared in 1970 in *The Birds Are Dying in Galilee,* in *Collected Works* (Beirut: Dar al-Awda, 1984), pp. 294–97. The lovers who make love by the window would kill each other outside it because they are enemies. Later in this segment of the text the poet echoes this line when he says, "Each of us is killing the other by the window," where the reference to killing is used, as elsewhere in the book, as a metaphor for the act of love.

Passion generated from passion. A rain that didn't stop. A fire that couldn't be put out. A body without end. A desire that lit up the bones and the darkness. We didn't sleep except to be awakened by the thirst of salt for honey and the smell of slightly burned coffee, roasting over burning marble. Cold and hot was this night. Hot and cold was that moaning.

I was stung by the heat of a silk that didn't wrinkle but became more taut as it rubbed against the pores of my skin and cried out. The air was like needles of warm spittle between my toes. On my shoulders an electric snake slid and craned its neck toward the embers. A mouth that devoured the gifts of the body. Nothing remained of language except the screaming of rooms wherein warring domestic animals were locked. Then sweat that cooled the air, making us shiver.

(*Each would kill the other outside the window.*)

| | | | | | | |

It's five in the evening here. I call out to the waiter, "Give me some more beer! Did S pass this way?" "I haven't seen him in two days." "And the lizard?" "She asked about him and left." "And the professor of ancient Semitic languages?" "He hasn't come in yet." "And the poet filled with eloquent emptiness?" "He left a little while ago." "And the professor of English at the American University?" "He came by in the morning." "And the retired leader?" "He hasn't shown up." "And the delegation from the International Red Crescent?" "They come and go." "Give me some more beer! Where's the Pakistani waiter?" "He comes at night."

Perhaps the woman sitting across from me has observed I've been stealing glances at her legs and so has stretched

them out, forcing them on my thirsty desire. I ask for more
beer.

| | | | | |

"It's five in the morning, my dear."

"And does the Arab get sleepy?" she asked playfully. "As for
me, I don't want to sleep."

I said, "Yes. The Arab does get sleepy, and tries to sleep."

She said, "Go ahead. I'll guard your sleep."

I said, "The lilac of your clear eyes will wake me up. Do you
realize your eyes can drive a restless urchin to worship stillness?"

She asked, "And what would they do to a man?"

I said, "Drive him to chivalry."

She said, "Go to sleep."

I asked, "Do the police know the address of this house?"

She answered, "I don't think so, but the military police do.
Do you hate Jews?"

I said, "I love you now."

She said, "That's not a clear answer."

I said, "And the question itself wasn't clear. As if I were to
ask you, 'Do you love Arabs?' "

She said, "That's not a question."

I asked, "And why is your question a question?"

She said, "Because we have a complex. We have more need
of answers than you do."

I said, "Are you crazy?"

She said, "A little. But you haven't told me if you love Jews
or hate them."

I said, "I don't know, and I don't want to know. But I do
know I like the plays of Euripides and Shakespeare. I like fried

fish, boiled potatoes, the music of Mozart, and the city of Haifa.
I like grapes, intelligent conversation, autumn, and Picasso's
blue period. And I like wine, and the ambiguity of mature po-
etry. As for Jews, they're not a question of love or hate."

She said, "Are you crazy?"

I said, "A little."

She asked, "Do you like coffee?"

I said, "I love coffee and the aroma of coffee."

She rose, naked, even of me, and I felt the pain of those
from whom a limb has been severed.

Silence.

Come back quickly! Come back, out of the aroma of coffee!
Something is missing from me. And I can't. I can't.

—What's gotten into you?

—Has it all come to an end?

—What's the matter?

—I can't get back to myself.

(*Each would kill the other outside the window.*)

—Take me to Australia.

—Take me to Jerusalem.

—I can't.

—And I can't go back to Haifa.

—What do you usually dream about?

—I usually don't dream. And you? What do you dream
about?

—That I stop loving you.

—Do you love me?

—No. I don't love you. Did you know that your mother,
Sarah, drove my mother, Hagar, into the desert?

—Am I to blame then? Is it for that you don't love me?

—No. You're not to blame; and because of that I don't love you. Or, I love you. My dear, my beautiful, my queen! It's now five thirty in the morning, and I must get back to them.

—To whom?

—To the Haifa police. I have to prove I exist, at eight in the morning.

—Prove you exist?

—And at four in the afternoon.

—And at night?

—At night they come without an appointment, just to make sure I exist.

—And what if you don't exist there?

—I'd be held responsible for any incident that took place in this country, for the Golan Heights all the way to the Suez Canal.

—And what's the punishment?

—Just my absence from the house means a five-year sentence at least. But for a bigger incident the punishment will be a life sentence.

—And what will you say in court?

—I'll say I was here, reliving the Song of Songs.

—Are you crazy?

—Crazy.

—And you don't love me?

—I don't know.

And each is killing the other by the window.

| | | | | | |

And there, in the far corner, I see the mare born from the praise poetry of the Arabs. A mare challenging the unknown, challenging language. A mare bursting forth from the drop of light shimmering over a field opened by the vibration of two strings of a guitar announcing the wedding of the knights it has wounded. Domes, minarets, towers, and space itself follow the shadow of the woman in love—a shadow moving toward the quivering spear. I'll turn my back to the daggers to fondle the moss of the mango and then fall into the great height of death, protected by mint and shrapnel that doesn't permit anyone to take even two steps in open space. Love means you hesitate. Love means that I become even more generous with the animals of the spirit. And love means I should hear only moaning from you. The air can turn solid, the sea can threaten if it wants, and you can cast the trappings of a fearful body into uttermost terror, to secure this fragile wooden door.

Come up one hundred and twelve steps, let your panting breath melt into a tired neighing, and let me wipe your sweat with a skin that has taken vows to perform just this duty. I shall call you D because you're the dawning of madness, the dawning of hell, the dawning of paradise, and the dawning of all passions that can win a war by an act of love not realizable except in the fear of death. Leave your daughter to play with the professor of chemistry, come over to this rocket observatory, and let us observe the cats in our bodies. Your foot is polished like a stone in the mountain rain, a stone that pierces my side till I let out a cry like wine in monastery cellars. And yet I don't cry out, lest you think anything aside from the siege can hurt. And I don't answer your greeting because I've conspired with my story against my passion for the first lock of hair to break me. For passion also has a mask, that the game may go on another year. I've grown tired of my mask, my game, and your fatigue. Therefore, stop pounding the stones of the street with a neighing that digs deeper into me. I've grown tired of traffic accidents not appropriate to this war, like the bumping of my left shoulder against your left shoulder in a childish encounter.

It's a shame we die of love in time of war. Do I love you? I don't love you if love lasts longer than the firing of a bullet into a spinal cord. And I do love you if love is surrender to a lightning storm that strikes me all of a sudden. Come over, that we may find the answer. Come, and let's ask the question. Nothing is left for those under siege in this last corner of the world but to let loose the genie of lust from the prison of words and gold. It is utterly unfair for us to part without having connected. And it is unfair to bring the look from halfway down the road back to an eye that pours honey over the fire. Your eyes can wound a stone, and in my blood they spread the sensation of ants crawling. When, then, am I going to gather these ants and return them to you, the house of ants, that I may stop scratching my blood with the sight of one leg on top of another.

Walk out the door and go left, then turn right. Go twenty meters, then turn left for thirty and take another right. There you'll find a huge chinaberry, a lone tree that will lead you to a small courtyard. Cross it and follow the aroma of cardamom to this building's entrance, like a shark chasing the smell of blood. Follow the cries of my blood and come up one hundred and twelve steps. You'll find the door open, and me on the other side, on fire with anticipation and ready for death standing with you, standing in you till we sit down when a rocket pulls us apart. Strike the stone steps as your high heels might rap on the edges of my heart, leaving a small piece for the dogs in the street. How I love high heels, because they stretch the legs into the totality of a femininity ready to break out! High heels contract the belly and open a curve for another belly shrinking from thirst. High heels lift the breasts, rounding them out and pushing them forward at passersby deprived of what they cheer for. High heels cast the feet into a readiness to dance over smoke rising from burning desire. High heels draw out the neck, like the craning necks of stallions at the moment of charging into an abyss. And high heels make the spear stand erect on a pulpit of solid air.

Stride the stones of the street with the pride of a gazelle not waiting to be received into someone's arms or his words. And slowly, slowly, materialize in front of the closed door. Behind it, there is a small leather settee to bear our weight, and big enough to hold us both. I'll sit first, then you. For the bedroom is exposed to the sea, which can see us as it shells and threatens. The living room is also open to the sea. And the library. Nowhere is left for us except this small settee. Tremble, shiver, and crumble, and don't take off your clothes, lest death see us stark naked. A mare in the lap of a man. There's no time except for quick love and a longing for transient eternity. No time for love in a war from which we can't steal anything beyond sucking up the sources of life itself. Is it part of the nature of war to create this lust? Is it part of the fear of death that it should quiver thus? Hands that scratch the wall to stop the cats from going away. And a mouth open to the sound of a wilderness too desolate to tempt wolves. I love this love in which there's no prattle or elegant words, and no slow putting on of clothes. In which there is no time for the rite that creates separation and slow disengagement from the embrace, and then the escape into the cigarette and the pretense of watching its circles of blue smoke, checking our watches, not to see the time but to find out when each must withdraw from the other. I love this love which leaves no pain in our memories or scars in our spirit. A love that enriches the soul with the rebellion of butterflies against the roses of the spirit. A passing moment that's more lasting and purer in its beauty than the bureaucracy of a long-standing love that needs a department for appointments and for keeping desire in good repair. A shudder which is the freedom of the poet in confounding the likeness between a woman and a song. A shudder which is the freedom of a silence liberated from another person with whom sharing a silence would be a solitude. Two worlds that don't impinge upon each other except through repression. In love there is no equality. Two worlds that return, when silent, to past memories more in conflict than in harmony. And I like making love on this settee that doesn't need to be made up because it doesn't wrinkle. I like it as I did when I made love on a rock by the seashore at night, or in a car hidden in a forest of willows, or on a night train in which names are not known, or during a long night flight, or by the fence of an athletic field in which the crowd applauds a speech while passing lovers also jump up down and cheer, but to a different climax. I like these moments/spasms, liberated from words and duties.

But the war invests this sublime furtiveness with the sufism of passion. How beautiful it is to die on the shore of the river of tart honey, without scandal, without nakedness, and without children! How beautiful to overcome the war within us with this fear that unites two bodies! And how beautiful to say farewell to our days with the opening of a rose that glows, moans, and tears itself apart with the friction of dew and salt under bombardment from sky, sea, and land—a shelling through which we guide the path of pleasure as it rises, mocking the barking of metal with the howls of flesh, blood, and taut nerves! Therefore, don't ask if I love you, mare born of Arabic poems of praise! Mare that dismounts from the lap of her knight to go back to her tender foal grazing in the midst of rockets, glasses of beer, the professor of chemistry, and the noble nurses from Scandinavia, come to exchange death from boredom and frustration for death for a cause. Don't ask if I love you, because you know how my body, searching for its safety in another body, worships yours. Take some bread and a bottle of water, so you can say you've been searching for bread and water for the past hour. You will be sung in my poetry because you didn't remain with me as did the Lily of the Valley, born from the Song of Songs. You will be visiting my poetry because you went away as she went away. And you will be born out of a dream that is born out of another dream, as the Lily of the Valley was born this dawn.

| | | | | | | |

The shelling shells everything. It even shells fear. In this far corner I'm thinking about the absent Pakistani youth. What brought him to this city from distant Asia? He was chasing after a loaf of bread, but the loaf trapped him in this siege. The loaf lured him from Lahore, made him run thousands of kilometers so he could finger this human miracle: a loaf of bread. A loaf of bread that may kill him in a war not his, and prevent him from going back anywhere, dead or alive, not even to a grave. *Vanity of vanities, all is vanity.* I consider the various ways to finish off a body that has struggled to attain maturity, only to burn or suffocate. *Vanity of vanities, all is vanity.* Keeping company with death has taught us that death has no sound. If you hear the hiss of the rocket, you're alive; the rocket missed you and hit another, like the Pakistani worker, for example. The rocket is faster than its sound. If you don't hear its hiss, know you're dead. *Vanity of vanities, all is vanity.* But what is the secret of this immunity? I feel a drowsiness that can't be resisted. A drowsiness more powerful than any power. An imperial drowsiness.

S wakes me up. He's armed with a long revolver and leaning on his emotional doll. "Where have you been?" "Where have *you* been?" *Sit with me if you can stop this lady's chatter, or else send her to any hell.*

—Where did you disappear to?

—The front lines.

—What news of the boys?

—Steadfast. Not worried about the outcome of the battle. They're holding on and fighting. But the people have grown weary, and it's said their steadfastness is tied to our leaving. Are we really leaving?

—Of course. Didn't you know we were leaving?

—I used to think we were just maneuvering. Are we really going to leave?

—We really are going to leave.

—Where to?

—To any Arab place that will accept us.

—Are they not ready for us to enter as we exit?

—Some of them won't even accept our corpses. The United States is asking some of them to agree to take us in.

—The United States?

—Yes. The United States.

—Do you mean that some of them want us to stay in Beirut and commit suicide?

—These are the ones who are not able to accept our resistance, but they're not calling for us to commit suicide, like the Libyan colonel. They don't want us to stay in Beirut, or in any other place on earth. They just want us to leave: to get out of Arabism and life, altogether out.

—Where to then?

—To nothingness.

—And when will we be leaving?

—After we get hold of some addresses where we can go. And after we get some guarantees to protect the civilians here and the refugee camps.

—Are there such guarantees?

—There are guarantees, and an international force will be arriving to protect the camps. But the Italian ambassador yesterday said something very worrying. He said no one can guarantee the Israelis won't enter Beirut after the fighters leave.

—Can't we keep the idea of leaving under cover, because it might affect the morale of the fighters?

—That's difficult, because the negotiators are making it known. And the Lebanese state itself is impatient, excusing itself with the need to calm the people.

—But why are we leaving?

—Because no one agrees to our staying: not the inside or the outside. Don't forget, the country is not ours and the period of hospitality is over. Even some factions in the Lebanese National Movement are now threatening us. There's no one left for us to depend on. No internal resources, and no support from the outside.

Of all people, S is the most anxious at the thought of leaving. He is terrified of becoming an orphan again. He is afraid we will forget him in the rush of these endings. He is one of hundreds of writers who had emigrated to the Revolution, which has become a home and an identity. He has nothing that can identify him: no identity card, no passport, and no birth certificate. That's why he finds in us, who have no homeland or family, a people and a homeland. Like Syrian, Iraqi, Egyptian, and Palestinian immigrants, he has projected upon Beirut a finality of meaning that grants their ambiguous relationship to the city the legitimate rights of a citizen, frightening many Lebanese, who know their city and society better than we do. They knew Beirut could not sustain all this projection. Some of them had already noted that the sense of easy relationship the city had inspired as a text open to writing and feuding had reached a degree of fragility that called for caution.

Yet Beirut was the place where Palestinian political information and expression flourished. Beirut was the birthplace for thousands of Palestinians who knew no other cradle. Beirut was an island upon which Arab immigrants dreaming of a new world landed. It was the foster mother of a heroic mythology that could offer the Arabs a promise other than that born of the June War. Each held on to what he cherished in the idea of a Beirut so fascinating that all had made mistakes, though she didn't enable anyone to define a comprehensive meaning for this fascination. Thus in the absence of the state apparatus that repressed citizens everywhere else, the link to Beirut became an addiction to language so metaphorical as to allow a claim of citizenship in Beirut, where one (anyone representing a state within this state) could carry on as he thought fit and turn this presumption upon the city into one of the forms of Arab training for an imagined democracy. Beirut thus became the property of anyone who dreamed of a different political order elsewhere and accommodated the chaos that for every exile resolved the complex of being an exile. To belong to Beirut thus became a reflection of legitimate opposition to Arab repression, and the refugee in the city no longer felt the need to worry about its collapsing order; rather, by allowing himself freely to form alliances within it, in the service of a democratic program addressed more to forces outside, he only helped speed up that collapse. Consequently, those living in Beirut, by allying themselves with the conflicting forces within, felt that a new standard had emerged for measuring citizenship and exile—a standard which defined even for the Lebanese, and with their support, the degree of their right to their country, because their homeland had been transformed from a republic to a collection of positions. In poetry as well, those who expressed love for Beirut were not Lebanese. When the Rahbani brothers sang for the homeland, they did not sing for Beirut. The song born of the civil war was "I Love You, Lebanon." Beirut was excluded because it had ceased to be Lebanon's Beirut. In the sectarian view, Beirut was not Lebanon; it had become Arab and was sung by the Arabs. It became possible for the poet of Lebanon, Said Aqel, to push Lebanese poetics to the furthest reaches of racist aesthetics when he wrote that the war was being fought, not between "the army of Lebanon and the army of Palestine," but against an entire people: "The Palestinian child is an enemy."

S and others had made up their own Beirut. They shaped it in their own image. They imposed themselves on the internal fabric of the cultural struggle, and when their cultural allies had shaken themselves off, they were left exposed.

Before the Israeli invasion many intellectuals, faced with the naked defeat looming on the horizon, took refuge in their sects and withdrew into their regional shells as a way of proving the failure of the secular project. There was a realignment of forces along sectarian lines, and the leading sect assumed the position of pattern maker. The hero of that sect, rising from the depths of crime, became the avowed model for representatives of other sects who imitated his pillaging. The poets of the status quo ante then rushed to the salons of East Beirut to obtain their Love-of-Lebanon indulgences from those wearing the fascinating mask of "Let's clear Lebanon of aliens." Destruction was in need of a state, and the fearful were in need of any state. Whereupon culture flourished in the eastern half of the city, now taking on the role of unifying the country. With a lineup of artistic acts, Casino Liban flourished. The only act missing was that of the Libyan dance troop, whose arrival was accompanied by the most deafening publicity. No one asked about the political significance of the Phalangist clamor for Libyan dances, for it was ironic and very clear.

When S, in the pages of the Palestinian literary journal *Al Karmel*, took issue with some intellectuals for giving up on the democratic program and returning to their sectarian shells, they accused the Palestinians of having become a Sunni sect. Poets, painters, and armed men fell upon us—as "representatives of a sect"—with threats and abuse because they considered our criticism of the intellectuals' return to sectarianism a slander against their sects. And when I swore that I never knew what my sect was, no one believed me, because the sectarian epidemic had already spread, and any attempt to understand what went on in Lebanon outside its limits was flawed. S used to defend his writings with muscles. He carried on with his visits to the coffee shops of Hamra, answering arguments by feeling his pistol. As for me, exposed to press campaigns, I never succeeded in proving my innocence of the crime of having said, "We are a part . . . We are not an island":

> The experiment is open to dialogue between thought and creativity, and we're still feeling our way to practicing the only choice open to us: creativity in the Revolution and revolution in creativity. We want to heal the damage inflicted by the current trend to separate revolution from creativity and set the two in conflict, with one party trying to create a divorce between literary expression and reality in order to arrive at a "pure literature," and the other pushing literature into providing a direct, daily service to the political program. We're a product of this reality and this time, in which vivid breakdowns are jumbled together with obscure births. We won't give up our dreams, regardless of how many times they're broken, and won't confront the crises thickening around us by dropping the Idea or by going for a pleasant stroll in our past heritage. Because we're not satisfied just to draw the line between crude oil and blood, we've chosen to believe that the future will be born—and only to the extent that we help in the delivery—from the present, not from the past, which in times of crisis is elevated to unquestioned authority. And when we note that the Revolution has not yet written its literature except in blood, we realize that the equation "words equal actions," linked within the context of the experiment, will mature to produce the new literature.
>
> We realize we're a part of the culture of the Arab nation and not an island within it. Therefore, we've never accepted our voice as the voice of a narrow identity, but see it instead as the meeting point for a deeper relation be-

tween the Arab writer and his time, in which the Palestin-
ian revolution will become the open password, until the
general explosion. We're not so much trying to form a
new movement in literature as to draw attention to a
wider context, or strategy, that would endow the idea of
Arab cultural unity with one of its possible forms (and
Arab culture is open to its diverse and multifaceted his-
tory) at a time when it is being exposed to more than one
effort to fragment it or strangle it at birth. Thus we don't
say that culturally the East is totally East and the West,
West, because we don't acknowledge just one East or one
West; and we don't wish to be imprisoned in a meaning
we ourselves didn't choose freely. We will have no com-
merce with those behind the current drive for resisting
Western cultural conquest (set into motion by a pamphlet
or two) unless it can be put in the context of a search for
an independence that rejects both subjection and break-
down, and only to the extent that they can tell one termi-
nology from another and avoid falling into a well that
shuts off the horizon. When we see the level to which
some aspects of culture have sunk and observe the control
of empty-headed and untalented sectarian parasites over
people's daily, weekly, and monthly nourishment, we do
not merely comment, "It's a crisis; better run." Rather, we
give the phenomenon its proper political address and pay
attention. We pay attention to literature's weaponry,
which is powerful enough to hide treason under the cover
of "disgust with politics"—that is, with having to strug-
gle—and also to claim sanctity and joy in dreaming.

No. We're not aliens in any Arab land. The aliens are
those who point to our exile with an accusing finger be-
cause they're strangers to their own history and the mean-

ing of their existence, strangers in a passing wave in which the thief can see nothing but the faces of other thieves. Yet if we can't be kind to traditionalism, we nevertheless are not content to accept the chaos of settling into an experimentalism with nothing to say beyond declaring its modernity. And if we complain of the general inability to perfect a language of the people in creative expression, that should not prevent us from insisting on speaking for them until the moment arrives when literature can celebrate its great wedding, when the private voice and the public voice become one. Yes. There is a role for literature, and severing the relationship between the text and those for whom it is transformed into power is the very alienation of letters which the prophets of the final defeat of everything are now extolling.

At this juncture, we cry out for help from criticism. We call upon it to regain its faith in its power and usefulness. We call upon it to enter the lists, now open for spoils. We call upon it to set down norms, the absence of which has opened the field for the ignorant and the counter-revolutionary to foist themselves off as moderns. We call upon it, for example, to reconsider the modern movement in Arabic poetry, which has found room for all sorts of wars but has now reached a crossroads leading to the loss of the illusion of its unity. And we call upon it to reject the sanctity claimed by a poetic text that allows no tool for its analysis except self-reference and, at the same time, reserves the exclusive right to load itself with all the ideology exterior to this claim that it can manage to disguise. Meanwhile, critic and reader are denied the right to reveal this. Let us then question the dictatorship of the text. Timidity or ignorance have taken us to the point where progress has become

afraid to declare itself. Worse. Flawless Arabic is now con-
sidered a form of backwardness, and correct meter, reac-
tionary. Clarity has become a fault, and having a message
and communicating it, a barbarism. In short, reaction,
equipped with all the tools of modern form, has been able
to stand to the left of anything, laden with a significance
derived from tradition.

Further, it has been able to pull others to its theses in
this age when the grand Arab meanings are in retreat,
when the stray sheep have returned to their sects, mystical
beliefs, and symbols. They've announced their repentance
for a lifetime lost on liberation movements that gave rise
to nothing more than unexpected headaches, and on the
Palestinian revolution in particular, whose costs proved ex-
orbitant during this period in which "petro-culture" (not
troubling to reveal the difference between its standards
and the ideology of its sources) invaded all platforms and
institutions devoted to culture and communication. In the
final analysis the destruction of culture and the cultured is
the only clear outcome of the phenomenon of the petrol
"patronage" of culture.

This is how the difficulty of the battle we're waging
over the question of literature is to be defined, and it di-
rectly or indirectly reflects the political and intellectual at-
tack of reaction, which is not short of reasons for taking
advantage of the failure of the so-called progressive re-
gimes that are in fact reactionary. And when we write, and
call upon others to write, in the name of creative freedom,
we are doing nothing more than bringing into focus the
points of light and first efforts scattered by dissension over
an idea founded on this simple assertion: we want to liber-
ate ourselves, our countries, and our minds and live in the

modern age with competence and pride. In writing, we
give expression to our faith in the potency of writing.
From this perspective, we don't feel we're a minority but
announce that we are the minority-majority. And we an-
nounce further that we are children of this age, and not of
the past or the future.[38]

Why did this discourse arouse their hysteria?
Because they wanted us to be an island under siege.

| | | | | | |

S asks for the tenth time, "Where will we go?"

"I don't know," I say. "There's an officer in the war room
responsible for deciding who has to go and where."

He says, "They might forget about me."

I say, "Perhaps."

He's afraid, so much so that he shouts down his chatterbox
of a companion, who knows everything and has an answer to
every question. "Shut up!" he scolds her in a Kurdish English
that makes her fall silent for twenty whole seconds, after which
she carries on with her chatter. She's a radio turned on, oblivi-
ous to any audience. She's worse than a siege. He quenches the
fire of his questions—questions that stem from his sense of be-
ing lost—in the illusion of her strangeness. He has colonized
her, like a boat or a shelter. Because of her, he has a sense of
belonging—to her, to whatever can support exile with strange-
ness—until he can find out where he is.

I find him a solution: "Stay with me."

---

38. Darwish's editorial for *Al Karmel*, no. 5 (1982).

He finds it good news: "Where?"

I say, "Here, in Beirut."

He cries, "Are you staying?"

I say, "Yes. I'm staying."

He says, "But I don't have a passport or an identity card. Fake. All my papers are fake. How can I stay? And where will I go?"

I say, "Where do you want to go? Sudan, Yemen, Syria, Algeria?"

He chooses Algeria.

I say, "You'll go to Algeria."

He says, "You know, I've never traveled even once in my life."

I say, "You'll travel a lot, my son. You'll travel a lot."

We used to drink in this small bar in years past. And during the siege we drank enough barley juice to make even the donkeys speak poetry.

—By the way, where are the intellectuals who are angry with us? We haven't heard their voices since the beginning of the invasion.

—They went to the south.

—To fight the conquerors?

—They missed their families. Some of them may yet become poets of occupied lands or poets of resistance.

—Do they still suffer from that complex?

—They'll never be rid of it.

—Why do they want to get rid of the model, then?

—To grow up. To kill the "father" and grow up.

—Do you look forward to any change in their writing?

—I don't look forward to anything.

—But they're innocent, and well-meaning.

—And model prisoners in contradiction with themselves.

—They'll grow up when they have more experience.

—In sectarianism no one grows up.

—They're not sectarian. They're orphans and afraid, and the passing wave of sectarianism is their defense.

—Why are they showing us their muscle then?

—Because we're alien. And because the state has started the process of formation. The Israelis will elect Bashir Gemayel president of the state.

| | | | | | |

"Our Lady of Lebanon, protect him for all Lebanon!" The barely audible prayer spreads like a prophet's tent, like the raised turrets of Israeli tanks. The Israeli secret habit has now become an open marriage. Israeli soldiers stretch out on the shores of Junieh. And Begin on his birthday eats a whole tank made of halva and calls for signing a peace treaty, or for renewing the old one between Israel and Lebanon. And he chides America: "We've made you a present of Lebanon."

What is this old treaty, now up for renewal?

It is a fact that Begin doesn't live in this age or speak a modern language. He's a ghost, come back from the time of King Solomon, who represents the golden age of Jewish history that passed through the land of Palestine. In Jerusalem,

he made coins as common as stones. He built the luxurious temple on a hill and decorated it with cedar and san-

dalwood, and with silver, gold, and dressed stone; and he
made the royal throne of gilded ivory. He struck a treaty
with Hiram, king of Tyre, who offered metals and master
craftsmen, and fished with him in the Mediterranean. Solo-
mon built the boats, and Hiram gave him the seamen; he
built the temple and ruled when he became king. His peo-
ple learned metalworking and the making of weapons
from the Philistines, navigation from the Phoenicians, and
agriculture, house building, reading, and writing from the
Canaanites.[39]

Begin has assumed the persona of Solomon, pushing aside
Solomon's wisdom, his songs, and his cultural resources. He's
taken only the golden age, hoisted on combat tanks. He hasn't
learned the lesson about the fall of the kingdom, when the poor
became poorer and the rich, richer. His only concern with Solo-
mon is to seek out the king of Tyre to sign a peace treaty. Where
is the king of Tyre? Where's the king of Ashrafiya? Begin freezes
history as of this moment, not seeing the end of the temple,
of which nothing remains except a wall for crying—a wall that
archaeology hasn't been able to prove Solomon built. But what
have we to do with the history of what came out of history? For
in the mind of the king of the legend everything has been frozen
as it had been, and since that time history has done nothing in
Palestine and on the eastern shores of the Mediterranean except
wait for the new king of the legend, Menachem, son of Sarah,
son of Begin, who will protect the Third Temple from the anger
within and without, in league with the king of Ashrafiya—
Bashir, son of Pierre, son of Gemayel.

39. Darwish provides no source for this quotation.

Fedayeen: basil and freedom.
By the roof tiles of a song,
The desires of a rising street
With a heroic tale of freedom,
Pledged to the burning ember.
It's revolution
Revolution.

Their trenches, the sea air
Their shadows crack the rock
Their song of songs:
Either victory
Or victory.
From them the Idea is born:
It's revolution
Revolution.

In their hands we were born
As a flower opens.
How often, oh, how often!
Will fathers be in sons reborn?
And the forest carry a seed?
It's revolution
Revolution.

| | | | | | | |

During these afternoon hours, the sky lowers, heavy with smoke, steel, and humidity. A sky winding down to the earth. The contests on the airwaves with the voice of Feiruz, the only trace left of a shared nation, signal nothing, or nothing shared, because the voice is altogether severed from its source. It has left its home for an abstract blue that doesn't speak to one's feelings at a time when war has transformed everything into detail. "I love you, O Lebanon!"—a declaration not heeded by a Beirut preoccupied with its blasted streets, now compressed into three streets only. Beirut is not creating its song now, for the metal wolves are barking in every direction. And the sung beauty, the object of worship, has moved away to a memory now joining battle against the fangs of a forgetfulness made of steel. Memory doesn't remember but receives the history raining down on it. Is it in this way that beauty, past beauty come back to life in a song not suited to the context of the hour, becomes tragic? A homeland, branded and collapsing in the dialogue of human will against steel; a homeland, rising with a voice that looks down on us from the sky—a unique voice that unites what can't be united and brings together what can't be brought together. Speech has run far, far away. It has taken its words and flown. This voice is not the voice of our torture, not the voice of madness.

In these afternoon hours the body finds it hard to carry its parts, and the spirit, hard to fly. It lies in heaps over the places of fear and indifference; it can't speak. And we sit, unable even to exchange glances. Beirut in August is not in need of new fire. Behind us is a school, now transformed into a hospital. The jets circle over it viciously. The professor of political science, who has come from the United States, says, "We're sure to be hit; let's go down to the ground floor."

It's difficult to wake up G; she's been sleeping for a month. I'm thinking she may have a diseased liver, but they say extreme fear drives the fearful to deep and continual slumber. Sleeping, she sleeps; waking, she sleeps; walking she sleeps; and eating, she sleeps. We envy her system of automatic protection. The ground floor is no safer than the sixth: if the building is hit, we'll be trapped under the rubble. The jets make more passes, and they fly lower.

Just to change the subject for the moment, I say to the professor of political science, "I think, Doctor, that the dialogue about the Open University is now closed." He says, "A whole phase of Palestinian and Lebanese national action is also over; and the experiment of the new Palestinian society in Lebanon is about to come to an end, too." "Where will the new phase begin?" I ask, and he answers firmly, "Not from nothing, as they claim. Not from a blank sheet, but from our store of experience. We've achieved much and must now develop what's worth developing."

We're no longer in a position to formulate a complete sentence, yet he'll have us reformulate the elements of an experiment that may crumble at any moment. The man's not uncaring. He's very concerned with his ancient origins, taking pride in roots pulled up forty years ago. He comes from Chicago once a year to feel the warmth of his people's renaissance. He's bored with his prolonged exile there, in a department of political science, and is now possessed by the idea of establishing an open university in Lebanon for Palestinian students who live in the Middle East. To criticize the validity of this idea and its efficacy is to attack his most precious dream and to change him into a mass of nerves as he defends his project.

The academic level was getting progressively lower at local universities. To get better grades, some students didn't hesitate to threaten their teachers with weapons. They entered the exam rooms armed to the teeth with handguns. We received many complaints, but no one was able to resolve the problem because of confusion about the identity of the factions. Before that, life was becoming more difficult for students who couldn't find Arab universities to accept them. I used to joke with the doctor, "In this setting, where we can't even control the conditions under which an exam is taken, do you really want to start an open university, which needs social stability and a different educational level?" But the doctor believed intensely in the reality of the idea and its feasibility. He saw our situation from a distance, and from that distance phenomena hide their details and show only their brightness.

—What's your project now?

—I'm going back to Chicago.

—And the Open University?

—It's closed.

Then descends upon us the American who appears when he should disappear. An American elated to see what he's seeing, a happy witness to experiences not available to others. War and siege. To an American who runs after any tragedy with a camera, a notebook, and a wife, is there anything more exciting than this death? I call him Cause-Man because he's a lover of hot issues. I'm not comforted by his fascination with a war that serves only to supply him with a wealth of material. More of us must die that he may have more to do and the excitement of sharing the life of the victim. He came all the way from New York just to watch us. He's not a professional journalist who runs after news in serving his profession. He's an amateur who records tragedies on tape with the lens of a video camera.

—How are you feeling?

—The opposite of you.

—What do you mean?

—What don't you mean?

—Will you recognize Israel?

—No.

The doctor was invited by the leadership to take part in formulating vague legal expressions for getting around that very question, which was one of the reasons for the present shelling. Vague expressions in relation to United Nations resolutions. The victim must concede the right of his killer to kill him, and those buried under the rubble have to declare the legitimacy of their slaughter. This would not have been the right moment for political rape, had the sadism not come in the form of jet squadrons. For the first time in our history, our absence is conditional upon our total presence. Present to make oneself absent, to apologize for the idea of freedom, and to admit that our absence is a right that grants the Other the right to decide our destiny. The Other, present with all his murderous gadgets, is demanding our presence for a while, to announce his right to push us into the final absence.

—Why are they demanding this recognition from us now?

—For your safety, and the safety of the world.

—A drowning man has no need to make sure the river is flowing. A man on fire has no need to make sure the flames keep burning. And a hanged man doesn't have to guarantee the strength of the rope.

| | | | | | |

I'm holding a bunch of grapes and two newspapers. The letter H descends upon me, afraid. She's always afraid—in peace and war—afraid of everything: a night without a lover, a year without a new book, a house with no piano, a month with no money, or a path with no dalliance. She swoops down on me like an accusation upon a thief: "When are you going to withdraw? When are you going to withdraw? You're destroying Beirut with this heroic absurdity."

I say, "You mean absurd heroism?"

She says, "No difference. Do you still believe?"

I say, "Do we still believe what?"

She says, "Anything. Leave . . . Leave, that water may come back to Beirut's pipes!"

She's always like that. Nervous, difficult, intelligent, stupid, and attractive like a sparrow. She considers water and perfume holy. She's every lover's first love, gentle and fragile. For twenty years the virgin of beginnings, yet she cultivates the undulating movements of her belly to seduce flocks of pigeons. She plunges headlong, then retreats. She licks her lover's foot with her tongue, washes his socks and his back, gives him a shave, offers him the day on a plate of chestnuts and the night on a bed of jasmine. But she no sooner takes the plunge than she mocks herself and her illusions: "I made a mistake. He's not worth it." We tease her, her family and I, referring to this humor of hers as George. "Do you remember George?" And she jumps out of her childish face to bite us one by one. We carry on laughing, and she with breaking the dishes.

I love the swing of her emotions, her devilish innocence, and her fear of the jets when they make her jump over the furniture like a grasshopper and shout: "Enough! Enough!"

Her father cries for any human being who dies anywhere. Her mother prays to Our Lady of Lebanon to protect her hero for all of Lebanon. Her sister prepares the food for a boy who's never full and waits by the phone for news of a certain young Frenchman. I carry on, apologizing for our presence in Beirut.

—When are you going to leave?

—When they stop the shelling, and the road to the port is safe. Calm down, H. It's not we who own these jets.

—How long will you carry on with something that's going nowhere?

—Take this bunch of grapes, and scan the papers for the names of the dead. They're shelling the old people's homes. They're even shelling our martyrs in the cemetery, restaging their death.

—Are you going, and leaving us your martyrs?

—If you can give me back what in your blood is mine, we'll take our martyrs with us to sea.

—I don't mean, I don't mean to hurt you.

—And we'll take the mist of mirrors, midnight dreams, and the songs of Feiruz about Beisan.

—I don't mean to hurt you.

—And we'll take the bread made of words.

—I don't mean to hurt you.

—And we'll take the smoke of burned hearts.

—I don't mean to hurt you.

—And we'll take the silence out of which poems rise.

—I don't mean . . .

—And we'll take the traces of a rain splattered on footprints that tried to give these times their real name.

—I don't mean to hurt you.

—And we'll take what we can see of the sea. We'll take it to sea with us.

—I don't mean . . .

—And we'll take the aroma of coffee, the dust of rubbed basil, and the obsession with ink.

—I don't mean to hurt you.

—And we'll take the shadows of the jets and the roar of the artillery in sacks full of holes.

—I don't mean to hurt you.

—And we'll take whatever memories are light to carry, titles for a heroic tale, and the opening parts of prayers.

—I don't mean to hurt you.

—And we won't take anything. We won't take anything.

—I don't mean to hurt you.

—We won't take anything with us. Take my bed, my books, and my sleeping pills. Take my absence, all of it. Take my absence from the settee by the door. Take the absence.

| | | | | | |

Did I cry? I oozed liquid salt in great quantities, the salt of the sardines which have been my sole diet for days. The jets can no longer make me disappear, just as heroism can no longer make me high. I love no one and hate no one. I don't want anyone and have no feeling for anything or anyone. No past and no future. No roots and no branches. Alone, like a tree deserted in the storm on an open plain. And I can no longer feel shame for my mother's tears or tremble at the crossing of two dreams born together at dawn.

| | | | | | |

Let Beirut be what it wants to be:
This, our blood raised high for her,

Is an unbending tree. I now wish,
I wish I knew where the heart will fly,
That I may release for her the bird of my heart
And from my body let him set me free.

I am not yet dead and know not if I'll grow
One day older, to see what can't be seen
Of my cities. Let Beirut be what it wants to be:
This, our blood raised high for her,
Is a wall holding at bay my sorrow.
Should she want it, let the sea be ours,
Or let there be no sea in the sea,
If that's what she wants.

Here, within her, I live,
A banner from my own shroud.
Here, I leave behind what's not mine.
And here, I dive into my own soul,
That my time may start with me.
Let Beirut be what it wants to be.
She will forget me,
That I may forget her.

Will I forget? Oh, would, oh, would I could
This moment bring back my homeland
Out of myself! I wish I knew what I desire
I wish I knew!
I wish I knew!

| | | | | | | |

A sunset for the sunset. The dark masses of cloud, sated with
gunpowder, are moving toward the edge of the sea. The birds
take up their fatigue and circle in the sky, searching for a safe

spot out of reach of jet wings. A sunset that signals what fatigue there is in us. Night, charcoal, and artillery shells come crashing down on us, that the body may long for another body that lights up a longing where there's no passion or death—a mechanical, metallic longing not penetrated by secret birds or a distant song, a longing carved from the tree of the unforeseen, just as dead time may long for a salty nut or a voice from the radio.

Where shall I go this sunset? I'm weary of this staircase here. I'm weary of that chatter there. Over there is the balcony of the poet who foresaw the fall of everything and fixed a date for his own end. Khalil Hawi took a hunting rifle and hunted himself, not only because he wanted not to give evidence against anything but also because he wanted not to be a witness for or against anything. He was weary of the state of decay, weary of looking over a bottomless abyss.[40] What's poetry? Poetry is to write this cosmic silence, final and total. He was alone, without an idea, a woman, a poem, or a promise. Was there anything left after Beirut fell under siege? Any horizon? Any song?

I played backgammon with him more than a month ago, and he didn't say anything to me. I didn't say anything to him, either. We just sat down and played. A game that needs no brains or strategy. Chance is the principal player. And chance had to obey Khalil Hawi, or else he was angry with it and with his opponent in the game. To win mattered a great deal to him. The opposite of poet A, who smiled whether he won or lost

40. Khalil Hawi was a prominent Lebanese poet who committed suicide on the second day of the invasion. For his poetry, see Adnan Haydar and Michael Beard, *Naked in Exile: Khalil Hawi's "The Threshing Floors of Hunger"* (Washington, D.C.: Three Continents Press, 1984).

because what mattered to him, what he bet against, was outside the game. Therefore playing against him was dull, unlike playing with Khalil Hawi, who was always enthusiastic, changeable, cursing and stabbing in his satires. I don't want to look over his balcony. I don't want to see what he did to himself on my behalf. The same idea has occurred to me many times, but either it retreated, or I did.

And near this balcony, four streets down, another poet fell not long ago. A poet who called himself the Wolf, the Gypsy, and the Lord of the Sidewalk. He was handing out his poetic identity, *The Sidewalk,* when he was hit. He was hostile to institutions, all institutions, and was setting up the institution of the sidewalk, his institution. But his rival on the sidewalk, his stubborn enemy R, said with pride: "I killed Ali Fodeh." "How did you kill him?" we asked. He said, calmly and rationally, "I focused my hatred on him. My hatred guided the shell to his belly. I'm the one who killed him." "Aren't you sorry?" we asked. "No," he said. "I hate him dead or alive, and I deserve to be congratulated."

| | | | | | |

Where shall I go at sunset? Guided by shells and light from the jets, my steps lead me to B's house. It may appear to those who don't know him that B is running the whole war—battle, negotiations, and information services. Spry, youthful, and a troublemaker, he found in this war his long-lost game. One hand on the phone, giving out statements about what he knows and doesn't know, and the other writing out orders, instructions, or advice. He handles twenty appointments an hour without getting tired. A beehive of a man whom fate has singled out for humming. A friend who sets no terms for friendship. Amusing, intelligent, and giving.

In his house there's an Idol that doesn't speak. An Idol cheered and worshipped. The quieter he becomes, the more the wisdom of his silence stirs up a storm of applause. And in the house there's a friend whose name is A, who can imagine what the world will be like a century and a half from now. His thoughts, which run along the lines of formal logic, arouse a cinematic excitement. He speaks of states large and small as he does of the streets of Beirut, without hesitation or having to be asked. And if his expectations turn out to be true, this Eastern region will in a short while be under siege by two types of priests of darkness. I agree with his forecast, deeming it the final stage of the ongoing disintegration and one of the forms of the coming catastrophe. But we differ endlessly about his claim that such an outcome is all that can save us, because one darkness can triumph over another and leave the dawn for us. Regardless of the extent to which the slogans of modern politics are severed from principle and its discourse emptied of content, I don't believe—I don't want to believe—that the history of this East will either mechanically repeat itself or bring about anything new. I don't expect Arab renewal to come except from the Arabs themselves. And I don't see that the model set up to tempt those who have despaired of this age with a return to faith has anything to offer short of going back to a struggle over questions no longer our questions. What have I got to do with the mistakes of Othman Ibn Affan since that history, by itself, is not my history?[41]

41. Othman Ibn Affan (c. 574–656), son-in-law of the Prophet and third caliph (644–656), belonged to the Omayyad family. His caliphate brought to the fore questions of political legitimacy that are still not totally resolved. He

A and B insist we're not going to withdraw, not because they lack information or aren't privy to the secrets of the negotiations, but because the idea of leaving Beirut is like that of leaving paradise, or one's homeland. It's most difficult for anyone who has taken part in shaping that experience, watching it grow from the beginning with his personal growth, to place himself outside it in the process of coming to terms with an ending that seems like a bolt of lightning. No one has prepared himself, not even in imagination, for such a proposition. Assuming the balance of forces will compel us to leave, what options have we readied to counter the prospect? How have we prepared to deal with what's going to be worse? What alternatives have we proposed to this concentration of institutions in one place? Have we been touched by a kind of fatalism and a reliance on sheer luck? Have we not already saved ourselves more than once? For how long then are we going to rely on having to save ourselves?

M is quiet, withdrawn, from us and the lizards. Enclosed within himself. He sees the sea. He sees us on the sea—as if he's just come out of my nightmare. No one pays him any heed as he effaces himself with silence and holds back the waves of the sea tumbling over each other in the room.

"Do you see something we don't see, M?"

"And do you see something I don't see, M?" he answers.

---

aroused the ire of the early Muslim community in firming up the power of the Omayyads, who through him could claim religious sanction for their control over the caliphate. Further, he recognized only one version of the Qur'an and suppressed all others. When the community rose against him, he refused to abdicate, saying, "I will not remove the shirt [Arabic qami:S] that God gave me." He was assassinated in Medina in his own house in A.D. 656.

I'm filled with fear.

"Did you see my dream? You weren't in my dream."

"I wasn't in your dream, but do you see what I don't see?"

The voices are suddenly quiet, as if to make sure we've gone mad.

He takes me to the veranda. "Is your apartment safe?" "What do you mean?" I ask. "Is it safe enough for the chief to sleep in?" he asks. "Are your neighbors with or against us?" "The sea itself is against us," I answer. "Do you mean you're afraid for his ship?" he asks. "I mean my apartment has a glass front, open to shells coming from the sea," I answer. "It won't do," he says. "It'll be better for him to sleep in a garage again tonight, or on the street."

"The breezes of paradise are blowing." So says the chief, who has readied himself for death and abrogated all commitments. There are no more possibilities for new characters to appear on the stage. He stands face to face with destiny. Is the tragedy Greek or Shakespearean? All the elements of theater have been stuffed into this long scene. Will he then sacrifice the child hostage, Beirut, or will he decide to leave for he-knows-not-where? Is he to die here in a great explosion so that the Idea may make known its prophecy, or will he rescue the structure by taking it to sea? Nothing is left here to rally what's beyond sea and siege. The whole world has scattered from the scene.

Alone. Loneliness without end. Was he alone from the very beginning without knowing it? Has he come early or late, this bearer of a matchstick in the oil fields? Alone, like a verse from a lyric with no beginning and no end. Alone, like the cry of a heart in the wilderness.

Some international organizations have already prepared

tents to help us through the coming winter. To them, we're still refugees who inspire pity and fear. And America still needs us a little. Needs us to concede the legitimacy of our killing. Needs us to commit suicide for her, in front of her, for her sake. Meanwhile, the Arab tribes offer us silent prayers instead of swords. Some capitals glorify their heroism in us but deny our sacrifice, for the fighter holding the line at Beirut airport is nameless. And some capitals have already prepared our funeral orations.

| | | | | | |

"The breezes of paradise are blowing." Will he reveal what he really thinks? Will he?

He won't.

I ask M, "Which sea will we cross?"

He says, "The Mediterranean, then the Red Sea."

I say, "Why are you so distant? Were you in my dream last night?"

He says, "I don't know. What dream?"

I explain:

We're in this very room: same conversation, same Idol, same air raids. The guard comes in to tell us a stranger who says he's an old friend has come to visit. Each of us fingers his pistol, in readiness for whatever mystery the door may open on. We hide the Idol in the bathroom. But the visitor turns out to be Izzeddine Kalak, intense and grinning as usual.[42]

"How did you get here?" we ask.

"As you came," he answers, "so did I."

---

42. Izzeddine Kalak was a Palestinian intellectual and the PLO representative to France. He was assassinated in Paris, presumably by the Israelis, in August 1978.

He hasn't changed at all. Distant, but genial. Yet he keeps staring at you, M, with the wariness of someone meeting a stranger for the first time.

"Don't worry, Izz," we say, "M's from the war room."

We talk with him, showing no surprise, as if he were an ordinary traveler just arrived from Paris. He shares his presence with us, taking part in the great communal separation from this place. We forget he'd left us forever ten years ago, that the dead don't visit the living except to raise doubts. Yet here's Izzeddine, with us, causing no confusion or fear.

I ask about his condition there, in the next world. He says it's normal; there's nothing new under the sun.

"Is there a sun there?" I ask.

"Yes," he answers, "there's a sun there."

I ask about the weather, and he says it's hot and humid, because the weather in August is hot and humid. I ask if they have our news there and if they're up to date on the siege. He says they follow the news, hour by hour, on television and are angry because they can't do anything to help us. I ask who may have come from here to give live testimony about what's going on.

"No one," he says.

"They shelled the martyrs' cemetery," I say. "Did any of the martyrs manage to get through to your side?"

"We didn't see any of them," he says.

"Where do you live?" I ask. "In paradise, or the fire?"

"What do you mean?" he answers, as if finding the question odd.

"Where did you come from?" I ask. "Heaven, or hell?"

"I came from there," he answers, "from the other world."

I look him over closely to see if there's any sign of his abode on his body, but find him normal and ordinary, just as he was when he left us: no traces of eternal suffering, and no signs of bliss.

"Is that all, Izzeddine? Is that all? Did you get married?"

"I haven't found the right one yet," he answers. "He who has no chance in this world doesn't have one in the next, either."

"How do you pass your time there?" I ask.

"As usual," he answers. "From my office to my rooms at the university residence, and from the lecture halls to the homes of the students. I often think of you when I take the train from Paris, standing up, and when I look out over Picasso's house and his famous she-goat, and when I go to the restaurant with all kinds of bread stacked along the walls. And I remember the Tunisian students who shouted this slogan when we celebrated the anniversary of the Revolution: 'Trample, trample, with our feet / Those who call for surrender!'

"And we cheered back: 'Trample, trample, with our feet / Those who call for surrender!' "

We turn to look at B but can't find him. He's busy protecting the Idol from the shelling.

I say to Izz, "Before we're formed, do we still need illusions in order to be formed?"

"It seems so."

"During this formative period are we in need of idols to worship in our search for models?"

"It seems so."

"And in this phase of the race between our blood and the

Idea," I ask, "and between the Idea and the Organization, do we still need rotten ink and hackneyed literature to prove ourselves?"

"It seems so."

"If the answer to that is, 'It seems so,'" I ask, "why then should we exchange Beirut for dishonor, and so on?"

"I don't know."

"How do people think over there?"

"Like you," he says. "Just like people over here."

"Izzeddine," I ask, "what are you doing here? Weren't you assassinated? Didn't I write your obituary? And didn't we walk in your funeral in Damascus? Are you alive or dead?"

"Like everyone here."

"Izzeddine," I ask, "suppose I tell you we're the living; does that mean you're dead?"

"Like everyone here."

"Izzeddine," I ask, "suppose I say to you we're the dead; does that mean you're alive?"

"Like everyone here."

"Izzeddine," I cry out, "what do you want from me?"

"Nothing," he says.

"In that case, leave me alone."

"It's time to go," he says.

"Where?"

"Where I came from," he says.

"Stay awhile; we'll go out together."

"My leave is over," he says, "and I must be getting back."

"Where did you come from?"

"I don't know."

Then he shakes hands with us, one by one, but gives you,

M, a meaningful look that draws you away a little. We embrace him at the door, where he vanishes like a fleeting notion. I run my eyes over the stairs but can't find him. He has blended with the rain of rockets. I can't find him anywhere. I look over the shrapnel from the shells, but I find no one. There's no one there.

Izzeddine has vanished.

"Does he really have to get back?" I ask them.

"Who has to get back?" they say.

"Izzeddine," I answer.

"And who's Izzeddine?" they mock.

"The man who was here just now," I cry out. "The man whose steps are still ringing on the stairs."

They look at me as if I were possessed, and I point to the seat his ghost had just sat in. "Here, here!" I say. "You all spoke with him. You embraced him."

But they don't believe me. They offer me a glass of water and a cup of coffee.

Can a man dream while sitting with others?

Can he dream and carry on a conversation at the same time?

| | | | | | | |

The sea glides closer to us. Autumn approaches the sea. August gives us over to autumn. Where then will the sea take us?

The story itself. I have yet to write it or forget it. The agony of writing and its endless privation: the story of the man who sat on a rock by the coast of Tyre for twenty-seven years. Is it not time for it to set me free? Is it not time for it to take me with it to the sea? But who can think of writing anything today? I'll copy it out one more time, just to practice writing, just to find my way to the sea.

I'd grown weary of asking Hani: "What name shall we give the man whose name we've forgotten? And when will you take me to the rock from which Kamal came down to go to the sea?"

"Who's Kamal?" Hani asked.

"The man about whose name I've been asking you for three years," I said. "The man who sat on a rock by the coast of Tyre, waiting for a dove to appear from the southwest, when the sky was clear and the sea calm."

He didn't know anything, anything, except the dove that no one else knew about. His eternal secret. If his friends in the refugee camp came back alive from sneaking across the border, or if they died, their heroism was all one to him. He sat on his rock, waiting for the time when he could ride the sea to the dove. It wasn't possible for raiding jets or even martyrs' funerals to pull him away from that rock. Only fog and sunset brought Kamal back to his family.

"Can a dove live for twenty-seven years?" I asked Hani.

"Kamal believed it could live from beginningless time to eternity," he answered.

"Why didn't he shoot it then?" I asked.

"Because it doesn't fly at all, and because he couldn't reach its nest," he answered.

Finally, Hani put his hands on the table and opened them, letting the secret out all at once:

"Why should I tire you, and myself as well, by keeping it to myself? There's no need for all these questions. The dove is Haifa. Because Mount Carmel, born out of the sea as it rises to the sky and the sky as it falls to the sea, is shaped like a miracle: I mean the city of Haifa—a neck constantly caressed by a ring of stone and trees, crowned by a sharp desire in the shape of a many-colored beak that affirms it is possible for a wild wave to turn into stone from beginningless time to endless eternity. Because it is like that, Haifa resembles a dove, and every dove resembles Haifa.

"But what Kamal didn't realize was that the city could fly. It was flying in his blood.

"Kamal withdrew into his secret, closing himself off in memories that had turned into dreams. He was constant in his devotion, pulling himself away from a time that didn't appeal to him and which he didn't recognize. Whatever went on in this age was a major or minor worry for someone else. Four wars had been lit. They weren't his wars, and he showed no concern so long as not one piece of their shrapnel could take him to the Dove."

"Give me more details about Kamal, Hani! Did you know him personally? Did you see his picture?"

Hani hesitated in giving an answer, and thus I knew he didn't have one, but he said, "He who watches the sea doesn't know the sea. He who sits by the shore doesn't know the sea. And he who comes only to look doesn't know the sea. Only he who dives knows the sea. He takes risks. He forgets the sea in the sea. He dissolves in the unknown, as he might in a lover. Nothing to separate the blueness from the water. And there you seize upon a world that words can't get hold of. It can't be seen or touched except in the depths of the sea. The sea is the sea."

"I don't like your poetry, Hani. Don't tell me about yourself. Speak to me of Kamal."

He couldn't. For three years, he'd been telling the story of himself and the sea at Tyre, and nothing of Kamal. Nothing except the place.

"Tell me, what's Kamal's story?"

"I told you he called Haifa his Dove, that he was a fisherman. He fished at night. During the day, he looked toward the Dove."

| | | | | | |

No one can follow a wave as it sinks into the sea. When the luckless lover comes out of his first love and suicide attempt, it's as difficult for him as for a judge to prove his innocence. Because the luckless lover prefers punishment to a confession that excites ridicule, he'll have to go to his first prison and follow a different path when he comes out. What if I'd said, "When I crossed the street over there, I wasn't carrying a bomb and wasn't aware of the sign that said 'Closed Area.' I was only carrying my heart's thorns to toss into the sea, because my sweetheart was going to be married that night." Or, what if I'd said, "Your Honor, I wanted to commit suicide in a watery unknown that gave no warning of pain. But the moon shone bright, and I saw the jagged edges of the stones under the clear surface of the water and was frightened. I came back because it was obviously going to be a death full of wounds from the rocks and very painful." *To hell with those who set the date of the wedding on a moonlit night!*

But if I'd said what I should have, to save myself from prison, would the judge have been able to see it my way? Would he have believed I was crossing this road to commit suicide for the sake of a young lady and not a country?

In this way the judge showed me there was another road to the sea. That the sea held another secret. And ever since that day, I've been coming to the sea but not seeing it.

"Do you know why you don't see it? Because you go only as far as the shore."

"But I do see the sea."

"No two people can know the sea the same way."

"What happened to Kamal? Is he still gazing at the Dove?"

"He went back to the sea. He went searching for the Dove."

| | | | | | |

Kamal was a man of few words. Almost mute. Perhaps he believed words would spoil the vision and disturb the Dove. Even so, he once sang:

In this camp
A rose is born.
If it lives too long
The Dove will be lost.

"What did he mean?"

"I don't know. He was obscure. As if he weren't one of us. The return wasn't the same to him as to us."

In autumn, the sea is not like the sea.
It's a carpet of water, and the light, like brocade.
In autumn, the bells of the sea are still,
Only the blood bells ring.
In autumn, the Dove wilts.
In autumn, the heart becomes a ripe apple.
In autumn, memory shatters,
And wine flows from forgetfulness.
In autumn, the mute speaks:

"I wish I could scatter my footsteps
Over a path of foam!
I wish I could scatter my footsteps,
And sleep on a bed of foam!
Haifa! Why don't you fly like a dove?
Haifa! Why can't I fly or sleep?
Haifa! Why don't you tell the truth:
Are you a city or a bird?
I wish I could scatter my footsteps,
And then rest forever."

| | | | | | | |

Kamal stole a boat.

He rowed in the direction of the Dove. When he approached, it was high noon, very bright. The Dove's feathers, embroidered with white poplars and clouds, were visible. The coast guard was also visible. He turned back to the open sea and pretended to fish till sunset, when he could leap out to the ring of the Dove, sleeping on the waves two minutes away.

He found his lost wave and introduced himself. When he had awakened twenty-seven years ago to the sound of bullets from the direction of the municipal building, he had opened the window and seen people converging on the port. He came down Abbas Street and sailed with others in the direction of Acre, which hadn't yet been occupied. And on that same wave, he reached Tyre.

It appears Kamal was happy with the way he had taken full possession of his destiny. He had taken hold of the moment separating two ages that do not meet. He had mastered the wave that took him into exile and was bringing him back now, like a dreamer waking up at just the right moment to put the whole

dream down on paper. Had it ever happened before that a sailor
came back on the same wave that had made him an exile and
had then vanished? Had it ever happened before that the one
who was slain killed his killer with the same stab of the dagger?
Had it ever happened before that someone returned by the same
path he had gone?

He never could disguise his mockery of the road others had
taken. He was not on a pilgrimage. He wanted to inflict the most
severe punishment on an age that had broken him. *He will row
calmly. He will land by the first rock. He will take hold of the boat
with both hands and plant it in the sand with the strength of all
the doves he had seen in other skies. He will kiss the dry earth and
scoop from it the aroma of a youth that had been broken and
scattered. He will reach for his mother's key, which he had taken
back from her tomb. He will walk the Avenue of the Kings, parallel
to the sea, and remember the first era of his life as a fisherman. He
will mount the ancient stone steps, beginning with the Steps of the
Maronites and ending at Khouri Street. He will turn to look at
windows under which he had picked up the disease of smoking and
learned his first whistles. He will then turn left toward the square
full of cats, from which he will descend five narrow steps and an
even narrower alley to find himself overlooking Wadi al-Nisnas
with its balconies hanging over the Greek Orthodox Church. He
will avoid looking in the direction of the eastern corner, which over-
looks a set of wide steps leading to the Jewish Quarter. He will buy
a fresh loaf of bread from the baker at the head of the Wadi. He
will mount a long set of steps on the right and greet the people
sitting on their balconies at ground level at the entrance to Haddad
Street. Arriving at the spot where three ascending streets cross the
steps, one of which leads to Abbas Street, he will mount, mount,*

and not pant. He will stand long in front of the bridge, to fill his lungs with the aroma of holm oak and flax. He will then walk seven steps, and the port and the sea will face him. He will sit on the old wooden chair and flirt with Tyre, which he can see in the distance, and will fall in love with it for the first time. He will place the key in the lock, but it won't open because of the thick rust. He will knock on his neighbors' door and greet them, sharing their joy at his safe return and apologizing for his departure in the first place. He will open the door to his house and rush to the tap to water his thirsty plants. He will lie down on the tiles of the house and sleep for hours, hours, hours. He will sleep forever.

Kamal woke from his short sleep. The sea was full of joy. He felt so free he was a grain of wheat, the sea was a fertile soil, and the waves were ears of wheat.

He looked at the coastline unfolding in the direction of his outstretched hand. He saw a diamond cutting the mountain, to fashion him a cradle quickly. *He will sleep on a small rise above the sea, higher than sleep itself. The sea will long for him. It will turn him into a bird made of stone. He will sleep in a little while.*

At sunset, Kamal rowed with an enthusiasm he hadn't known before. When he came close to shore, the Dove's searchlights were fixed on him. It took some time for him to realize that he was surrounded by the boats of the coast guard, with guns aiming at him from every direction, that it wasn't the light of the Dove that had dazzled him.

A ripple rose in the wave.

A ripple rose in the heart.

—Do you have any weapons on you?

—I have a longing that's killing me.

—Where are you from?

—From the Dove.

—Where are you going?

—To the Dove.

—What's this Dove?

—Haifa.

—Who sent you?

—A thread of blood.

—How old are you?

—A wave that comes back and gets lost.

—Where do you live?

—In Tyre.

—What do you do there?

—I manufacture gods.

—What are the names of your gods?

—The Dove.

—Are you a fedayee?

—No.

—What do you want?

—I want to bury my body with my own hands within the ring of the Dove.

The men of the coast guard didn't understand or believe what he said. They thought he was maneuvering. Very cautiously they boarded his boat. They tied him up, removing his clothes. But they found nothing. No weapons, no identity card. They asked if he was a fisherman who had got lost at sea. "No," he said, "I'm not lost. I know the Dove very well, and I came to see the Dove."

—Is that all there is to it? You just want to see the Dove?

—Yes.

—Then you will see the Dove.

They nailed his hands, feet, and shoulders to the wood of the boat, and they said, "Stay here, and look at the Dove. The Dove is in front of you."

He bled, and the Dove got smaller and bigger.

A week later, the sea brought his body back to the coast of Tyre, back to the rock where he used to gaze at the Dove.

Can this be the sea?

Yes, this is the sea.

| | | | | | |

I come into the dark blue night of the city, heavy with fatigue and waking nightmares. My life has taken sharp turns. I can no longer carry on with these time shifts, and I can go no deeper than the beginning of the night. Who has brought me to the alley between the Mayflower and Napoleon? I won't go in there, for I already know by heart what I'm going to hear. The jets' flares light wide paths in the alley for my dragging footsteps. Here, I didn't die. Here, I haven't yet died. I've been dragging my shadow over this sidewalk for the past ten years, placing a signature on my exile, feeling sure I wouldn't be staying more than one year.

The years piled up, one on top of the other. For ten years now I've been knocking on this door, avoiding the sea. I used to prefer the land route, the path I walked thirty years ago and walked again to go back *there*. Did I forget to return, or did I forget to remember? How was everything, anything, ten years ago? My days march before me like sheep that don't belong to-gether in a herd. They march like the scent of a rose standing in the wind. They march before me as I'm now marching around them in a game of musical chairs led by metallic machines.

Here, I didn't die; I haven't died yet. But this howling that descends from the sky and rises from the earth doesn't stop. It won't permit any of the images of my days to settle into a form. It won't allow my fear to become whole or my recklessness to stay heedless. Enough! I move my hand in the lit darkness to chase the cloud of jets from my sight as a person might chase away flies. Enough! I say it louder. But the answer comes back louder and louder. The cloud spits masses of fire that bring me back from a journey on the train from Haifa to Jaffa, and I realize I'm now walking another road. Enough! I get the message. So what if I'm here? Here, I didn't die; I haven't yet died. Enough! We said we were going to leave, so why this hellish racket? Enough! Let's not leave, as long as they carry on with their hellish racket. Enough, you sons of bitches, fascinated with muscles of metal, laser beams, cluster bombs, and vacuum bombs! Enough of this unbridled show of strength! Enough chomping of the city and our nerves!

Darkness spreads quickly in a city without electricity. A single piece of charcoal can give birth to all this darkness in less than half an hour. The first part of the night tastes bitter, sour, flat. A taste that creates in the soul a country strange to be a stranger in, and in the hunger of a moist body it creates a languid longing for the hunger in another moist body. Forgetfulness leads to another pathway: "Each will kill the other outside the window."

The coast train raced against the sea on the right; and on the left, against the trees. Rain. Rain and trees. Rain and trees and metal. Rain and trees and metal and freedom. My naughty friend made endless fun with my thin, gloomy friend. For the first time they'd given us permission to leave Haifa, but we had to be back at night to report to the police station at the edge of the park, the city park: for each to say in his way, "Put this in your record: I exist!" "Put this in your record!"—an old rhythm I recognize! "Put this in your record"—I recognize this voice, whose age was twenty-five. Oh, what a living time! Oh, what a dead time! Oh, for a living time rising from a dead time! "Put this in your record: I'm Arab!"[43] I said that to a government employee whose son might now be piloting one of these jets. I said it in Hebrew to provoke him. But when I put it in a poem, the Arab public in Nazareth was electrified by a secret current that released the genie from the bottle. I didn't understand the secret of this discovery, as if with the gunpowder of identity I had stripped the minefield of its thunderbolt. This outcry then became my poetic identity, which has not been satisfied with pointing to my father but chases me even now.

I didn't realize it was necessary to say it here in Beirut: "Put this in your record: I'm Arab!" Does the Arab have to say this to his fellow Arabs? Oh, what a dead time, oh, what a living time! I glance at my watch to find out how old I am now. I'm ashamed of this glance: does a person have to look at his watch to know how long he's lived? A few weeks ago, my friend A set

---

43. "Put this in your record," is the first line of "Identity Card," one of Darwish's earliest poems. It appeared in 1964 in his first volume, *Olive Leaves*, in *Collected Works*, pp. 73–76. This is the opening stanza of the poem (my translation):

Put this in your record:
I'm Arab
Identity card number fifty thousand
My children are eight
And the ninth
Is arriving next summer.
Does that make you angry?

me up for an ambush at forty. At the birthday party, Mu'in laughed out loud: "You're no longer a youth, thank God! We're now rid of another youth. You're no longer a youth! You're now forty years old!"[44] I said, "What's making you so happy, old man!" "What makes me happy," he answered, "is that you're now forty." "But have you forgotten you're approaching sixty?" I asked. "That doesn't make any difference," he answered. "All ages are equal after forty. You've now caught up with me. For twenty years I've been waiting for you on the threshold of forty, and now you've arrived. Welcome! You're no longer a youth. No longer." Mu'in drank till he raved, till he thought that I was older than he, and that he had stopped aging. He was utterly fascinated by the parity. "Long live parity!" we cried out and celebrated with him.

| | | | | | |

Alas for the time! The train cuts off the sea from the trees. Trees and sea run away from the train. The train of age on the metal tracks of time. Was I really in my twenties when my identity brought me to that lyric hammered into shape by hooves disappearing into one horizon open to another, itself open to yet another horizon, open or not we didn't know? And was I really twenty-seven when that lyric came into contact with the Song of Songs and lit a fire in the Lily, and I heard the last cries of a horse that led the way from Mount Carmel to the Mediterranean? How long will pain remember the snake that put a spell on him, and how long will we go on reaching forty?

44. Mu'in is Mu'in Bseiso, a well-known Palestinian poet and Darwish's good friend, who died in 1984. His *Collected Works* (through 1979, Al-'a?ma:l al-Shi?riyyah al-Ka:mila), was published in Beirut by Dar al-?Awda, 1987.

A coincidence.

No more than a coincidence that the exit from the body should also be the exit from the country. I didn't remember this coincidence till this moment. A train and rain and trees, a space heater and two bare white feet on the skins of twenty sheep that passed through the Song of Songs. The singer was singing to Suzanne, who took him down to the river. She was saying, "Take me to Australia." And I said, "Take me to Jerusalem." No. I don't remember anything; I'm dreaming. Is the dream then what forgetfulness chooses? But out of one dream, another dream is born.

Are you alive?

Oh, for the time that lived! Oh, for the time that died! The circle is now complete. My mother, far away, opens the door to my room and offers me coffee on a tray made of her heart. I jest with her, "Why did you let me put my knee on the knife and press down so I would carry this scar? And why did you let me ride the horse whose bridle was going to come off, making me fall and leaving this scar on my brow?" The dark blue night is opening up, bringing release, turning white. Darkness is white, pitch-white.

| | | | | | |

I find myself sitting on a comfortable leather settee, listening to the harmonious triad of death: jets, navy, and artillery. I light a gas lamp to prepare my last rites. It's still only ten o'clock. I carry the lamp with its familiar snore and walk over to my study to write my will. I find nothing to will. There's no secret in my life, no secret manuscript, and no secret letters. My publisher is known. My life is the scandal of my poetry, and my poetry is the scandal of my life. An opening line, coming from neighbors' roofs, flutters into my awareness: "The doves are flying. The doves are landing. The doves are flying. The doves are flying."[45] I find it amusing to die at forty, not before or after.

I hear two raps on the door. She's there, tense, like a final call—the one obsessed with putting out the salt burning in her blood. I call her by another name. "Who's that?" she asks. "No one," I answer.

She takes the lamp and goes in search of the other name in every corner of the house and the balcony. She finds no one.

—Are you raving or dreaming?

—A little of this, a little of that.

—Who is she?

—No one.

—Are you in your right mind?

—Sometimes.

She approaches me and lights the fire of her soft belly. A fire blue and white. A snake's hiss. The whispering sound of salt. The repressed moaning of cats. And a desire for a different death.

—Every day?

—Every day till the siege is over, I go home, and you leave Beirut. Be my coffin, that I may be yours.

—On the balcony, then. I want to lift up my coffin on the balcony, within sight of their jets, boats, and artillery. Within sight of the lights of Ashrafiya.

—Are you crazy?

45. "The doves are flying / The doves are landing" are the first two lines of Darwish's "The Doves are Flying," which appeared in *Sea Elegies under Siege.*

—Crazed by life.

—No, not on the balcony.

—On the balcony you'll lift up your coffin. The balcony is life's defiance of death. It is resistance to the fear of war. I don't want to be afraid. I don't want to be ashamed.

—But can I let out a cry on the balcony?

—Must you always cry out?

—Men don't understand women.

—Women don't understand men.

And here, I didn't die. I haven't died here yet. Ten years I've lived here. I've never before lived in a place for ten years. I had never before got used to vegetable smells, vendors' calls, noises from the armed tavern, and problems with water and the elevator as I have here. Here, I didn't die. Many balconies overlooking many other balconies, open in spring, summer, and autumn, and in winter, early and late, to exchange secrets and petty scandals and loud television sets and the smells of garlic and broiled meat and the sounds of beds shaking afternoon and night. A small street—small, with the name "Yamoot / He Dies." And here, I didn't die.

A little while ago, in the season of car bombs, I was walking with a neighbor in the early evening when we heard a rustle coming from a car. We alerted the neighborhood that it was necessary for people to evacuate their homes until the military expert arrived. The explosion of a single car could have killed the inhabitants of the entire quarter, and they had come from all zones of massacres and sects, seeking shelter in the neighborhood of the American University. But when the military expert arrived and inspected the car, he found, not a hundred kilograms of dynamite as we'd suspected, but a rat gnawing the car's innards. People laughed when they realized that a rat had the power to evacuate an entire quarter. Yes, a rat has the power to evacuate a city and to rule a country.

And here, I didn't die. Here, I haven't died yet. Every time a plane lands at Beirut airport, I smell the scents of the unknown and the aroma of the coming departure. The fog rising from the summer's humidity and the cutting, harsh early dryness of spring awaken in me the sensation of the temporary. Are we going to stay here? We're not going to stay. It appears that the ending of things has a definite shape, a defined ambiguity, a collusion between nature and fear, particularly in August. August, the low, mean, aggressive, resentful, treacherous month. August, capable of supplying the symbol with all the corpses it needs and providing the body's lassitude with whatever steamy gloom or flushed and congested humidity nature may wish to piss on it. August's face is the face of one ready to burst but unable to find a urinal or an unobserved wall. The month of August is dirty, boring, arid, and murderous; it favors endings with long beginnings, endings that don't begin or end. It's as if August were the very sect of seasons that hasn't yet found followers. August is able to provoke even the sea—the sea that carries the whistle of bullets to the horizon.

—Tell me, Brother Mahmoud, what do you mean by "the sea"? What is the meaning of "the sea," in "The sea is your last shot"?

—Where are you from, brother?

—From Haifa.

—From Haifa, and you don't know the meaning of the sea?

—I wasn't born there. I was born here, in the refugee camp.

—You were born here in the camp, and you still don't know the sea?

—Yes, I know the sea. What I want to know is, what's the meaning of the *sea* in poetry?

—The meaning of the *sea* in poetry is the same as its meaning at the edge of land.

—Is the *sea* in poetry the same as the *sea* in the sea?

—Yes. The *sea* is the sea—in poetry, in prose, and at land's end.

—But they tell me you're a symbolist poet, overflowing with symbols. For that reason, I thought that your *sea* was not the same sea we know, a *sea* other than our sea.

—No, brother. They deceived you. My *sea* is your sea, and your sea is my *sea.* We came from the same sea and are heading to the same sea. The sea is the sea.

The fighter is amazed by the poet's inability to explain his poetry. Perhaps he's amazed by poetry's simplicity, so long as the *sea* is the sea. Or perhaps he's amazed that plain facts have the right to speak.

—Is it not you, brother, who bring the *sea* into poetry when you carry it on your shoulders and place it wherever you like? Is it not you who open wide in us the sea of words? Are you not yourself the *sea* of poetry and the poetry of the *sea?*

—I'm innocent. I'm merely defending my right, my father's memory, and I'm fighting against the desert.

—Me too. But the sea, brother, is the sea.

And to it we shall be going in a short while, in Noah's

modern arks, on a blue that reveals an unending whiteness that shows us no shore. Where to? Where in the sea shall the sea take us? And here, I didn't die. I haven't yet died.

I'll try to sleep now. What's sleep? What's this magical death spread with the names of the vine? A body, lead-heavy, is thrown into a cotton cloud by sleep. A body that soaks up sleep as an uncared-for plant absorbs the scent of the dew. I go into sleep slowly, slowly, to the rhythm of distant sounds, sounds arriving from a past scattered over the wrinkles of the days and my bed. I knock on the door of sleep with muscles alternately tense and lax. It opens its arms for me. I ask permission to go in, and it is granted. I go in. I thank it. I praise it.

Sleep is calling me, and I'm calling it. Sleep is blackness gradually crumbling to white and gray. Sleep is white. A separation, and white. An independence, and white. Soft, strong, and white. Sleep is the waking of fatigue, and its last moan; and it is white. Sleep has a white earth, a white sky, and a white sea; and strong muscles, muscles made of jasmine flowers. Sleep is master, prince, king, angel, sultan, and god. I abandon myself to it as a lover abandons himself to the praises of his first love. Sleep is a white charger flying on a white cloud. Sleep is peace. Sleep is a dream, born out of a dream.

Are you alive?

In a middle region between life and death.

Are you alive?

How did you know I was just this moment laying my head on your knee to sleep?

Because you woke me up now, when you stirred in my belly. Are you alive?

I don't know. I don't want to know. Does it often happen

that I am awakened from one dream by another, itself the inter-
pretation of the dream?

 That's what's happening now. Are you alive?
 As long as I'm dreaming, I'm alive; the dead don't dream.
 Do you dream much?
 When I'm approaching death.
 Are you alive?
 Almost, but in time there's room for death.
 Don't die.
 I'll try not to.
 Did you love me then?
 I don't know.
 Do you love me now?
 No.
 Man doesn't understand woman.
 And woman doesn't understand man.

No one understands anyone.
 And no one understands anyone.
 No one understands.
 No one . . .
 No one.
 The sea is walking in the streets. The sea is dangling from
windows and the branches of shriveled trees. The sea drops
from the sky and comes into the room. Blue, white, foam,
waves. I don't like the sea. I don't want the sea, because I don't
see a shore, or a dove. I see in the sea nothing except the sea.
 I don't see a shore.
 I don't see a dove.